BROWNIE GIRL SCOUT

HANDBOOK

Girl Scouts of the U.S.A.
420 Fifth Avenue, New York, N.Y. 10018–2702

GIRL SCOUTS OF THE U.S.A.®

B. LaRae Orullian, *National President*
Mary Rose Main, *National Executive Director*

Inquiries related to the *Brownie Girl Scout Handbook* should be directed to Program, Girl Scouts of the U.S.A., 420 Fifth Avenue, New York, N.Y. 10018-2702.

© 1993 by Girl Scouts of the United States of America
All rights reserved
First Impression 1993
Printed in the United States of America
ISBN 0-88441-279-2

10 9 8 7 6 5 4 3 2

CREDITS

Authors
Karen Unger Sparks
Sharon Woods Hussey
Chris Bergerson
Martha Jo Dennison
Candace White Ciraco
Toni Eubanks
Verna Simpkins

Contributors
Judith Brucia
Robyn J. Payne

Designer
The Antler & Baldwin
Design Group

Design Coordinator
Kristine Schueler

Illustrators
Pat Dypold, Cover
Fanny Berry
Judith Cheng
Michael Hostovich
Robert Lawson
Ben Luce
Susan Melrath
Linda Reilly
Claire Sieffert
Cornelius Van Wright

Contents

Welcome to Girl Scouts   **7**

The Story of Girl Scouting   7
More About Girl Scouting   12
The Girl Scout Promise and Law   14
The Worlds of Interest   16
The Brownie Story   17
Special Girl Scout Ways   22
Girl Scout Ceremonies   23
Girl Scouting's Special Days   24
Brownie Girl Scout Uniform   26
Brownie Girl Scout Insignia and Recognitions   28
Girl Scout Age Levels   30
Investiture or Rededication   31
Bridging   31
Girl Scout National Centers   32
World Centers   32
Brownie Girl Scout Scavenger Hunt!   32

Taking Care of Yourself and Your Home   **33**

Marisol Starts a Club   33
Taking Care of Yourself   36
Caring for Your Clothes and Home   42
Staying Safe   48
First Aid   58
Feeling Good About Yourself   62

Family, Friends, and Neighbors 69

Marta Makes a Choice 69

Family 72

Friends 75

Your Neighbors and Neighborhood 84

People Near and Far 87

Ananse's Gift 88

Ananse Guides in Ghana 91

Bluebird Girl Guides in Thailand 92

Alita Girl Guides in Peru 94

Grønsmutte Girl Scouts in Denmark 98

Games from Around the World 100

Art from Around the World 102

Storytelling 104

More About People 108

The United States of America 109

People Different from You 109

Leadership in Girl Scouting and Beyond 111

Brownie Girl Scouts Make a Difference 111

Getting Involved in Brownie Girl Scouts 115

Citizenship 115

Goal Setting 117

Leadership and Troop Government 119

Leadership and Troop Money 121

Girl Scout Cookies 122

Leadership and Group Planning 123

How and Why? 125

Kelsey's Computer Lesson 125

Brain Power 128

Science Is All Around You 132

Weather 137

My Natural Environment 144

Outdoor Skills and Adventures 148

Brownie Girl Scout Try-Its and Bridge to Junior Girl Scouts Patch **161**

Sara Joins the Troop	161
About Try-Its	164
Animals	166
Around the World	169
Art to Wear	172
Building Art	175
Careers	178
Caring and Sharing	180
Citizen Near and Far	182
Colors and Shapes	184
Creative Composing	189
Dancercize	191
Earth and Sky	194
Earth Is Our Home	196
Food Fun	200
Girl Scout Ways	202
Good Food	205
Her Story	208
Hobbies	210

Listening to the Past	212
Manners	214
Math Fun	216
Me and My Shadow	218
Movers	220
Music	225
My Body	228
Numbers and Shapes	231
Outdoor Adventurer	234
Outdoor Fun	237
Outdoor Happenings	240
People of the World	243
Plants	244
Play	246
Puppets, Dolls, and Plays	248
Safety	252
Science in Action	255
Science Wonders	258
Senses	262
Sounds of Music	266
Space Explorer	269
Sports and Games	272
Water Everywhere	275

Bridge to Junior Girl Scouts	*278*
Looking Back and Looking Ahead	*281*
Index	*284*

Welcome to Girl Scouts

"Okay, girls, I'll see you next week. Please remember to bring your permission slips for the camping trip," Mrs. Carreras said as we left the school cafeteria.

Later that night . . .

"I can't wait to go camping!" I said as I climbed into bed. "My first overnight trip! I know I'm going to have a great time!"

The Story of Girl Scouting

Oh, hi! My name is Jessica and I am a Brownie Girl Scout. At our meeting tonight, we had a party. We sang songs, played games, and listened to a story! After we listened to the story, Mrs. Carreras, our leader, told us she knew a woman who loved stories and Girl Scouting as much as we did. She was born on October 31, 1860.

Do you know whom Mrs. Carreras was thinking of? If you do, you could write her name here.

_____

That's right! Mrs. Carreras was thinking of Juliette Gordon Low, the woman who started Girl Scouting in the United States in 1912. Mrs. Carreras said that "Miss Daisy" was just like us in many ways. And you know what? She really was! Here's her story. See if you agree!

The Story of Juliette Gordon Low

When Miss Daisy was born, an uncle said, "I bet she's going to be a daisy!" And Daisy became her nickname among her family and friends.

Daisy lived in Savannah, Georgia, with her mother, father, her older sister, Nellie, two younger sisters, Alice and Mabel, and with Willy and George, her two younger brothers. Daisy was born during the time of the Civil War and members

of her family fought on both sides.

As a young girl, Daisy liked to do many of the things you and I like to do. She loved to use her imagination to make up her own games. She enjoyed swimming, playing outdoors, making paper dolls, and acting in plays. She'd even write her own plays and star in them!

She wrote to her grandmother, "I never felt better in my life. My complexion has cleared up. I take so much outdoor exercise that I'm

never tired!" In the same letter, she wrote, "Wish Alice happy birthday. Tell her to look in my paper dolls, and choose five as my present to her!"

What are some of your favorite things to do?

_____

_____

Daisy had great adventures with her brothers and sisters! Once, Daisy was making a kind of candy called taffy at her cousin's house. One

cousin, named Rudolph, noticed that the taffy was the same color as Daisy's hair. "Let's braid some into her hair," he suggested, and Daisy, always willing to try something new, agreed. Can you guess what happened? Well, the taffy became very hard and sticky, sort of like chewing gum, and Daisy's mother had to chop all of Daisy's long, beautiful hair very short to get rid of the sticky mess!

Daisy loved animals. One time she was worried about a cow getting cold. In the middle of the night, she took her mother's bedspread to the stable and pinned it on top of the cow. Her mother was not very happy the next morning because the cow had stepped all over the bedspread when it fell off!

Studying was never so easy for Daisy, but she loved her drawing classes. Once she wrote her mother, "Dear Momma, Please let me stop school. I hate it so and I don't believe I learn a thing!" Her friends who went to school with her said that

she worked hard, but she also liked to have fun. Daisy's mother believed that education was really important. School stopped at the eighth grade in Savannah, so Daisy and her brothers and sisters all continued their high school educations away from home at boarding schools.

When Daisy finished school, she moved back home to Savannah. She went to a lot of parties and at one of these parties, she met an

Englishman named Willie Low. Daisy and Willie were married and moved to England. She became friends with famous people like Rudyard Kipling, who wrote the *Just So Stories*, and she spent a lot of time drawing and painting. She also made her own blacksmith tools and made a set of iron gates. Her arms got so strong that she had to make the sleeves on her dresses bigger!

Daisy did not have children of

her own but she always enjoyed doing things to help young people. She particularly liked to help kids who seemed not to get much help from other grownups. On her trips to places all over the world, such as Egypt and India, she would bring along one of her nieces or nephews. She always had wonderful stories to tell about her adventures and would bring home bags full of special presents for everyone.

What are some ways you could help kids younger than you?

_____

_____

But, like most people, Daisy had a life that was not always easy. She had many troubles with her health. Daisy had problems with her hearing. She had an accident that hurt her good ear and afterwards she was almost completely deaf. She also did not have a happy mar-

riage with Willie. When Daisy was 44 years old, Willie died. But Daisy refused to let her problems stop her from doing things with her life that she wanted to do.

A few years later, Daisy met a very interesting man named Sir Robert Baden-Powell. He told Daisy all about an organization he had started for boys called Boy Scouts. Six thousand girls also signed up, so, with his sister Agnes's help, the Girl Guides were started.

This idea of a girls' movement really excited Daisy and she offered to start a troop in Scotland. Girls who were poor often did not have a chance to go to school. Usually, they would work in a factory. Factories were noisy, dirty, and very unhealthy. Daisy found a woman who could teach her and the girls in the troop how to spin cloth. They sold the cloth at a market in London and then used the money to start an egg business. The egg business was so successful that the girls could help their families with the money

She really was a lot like you and me because I know I have dreams that I hope to make come true. What are some of your dreams?

_____
_____
_____
_____
_____
_____
_____

and not have to work in a factory. Daisy wanted girls everywhere to be part of this organization. She formed troops in London and then made plans to come to the United States.

On March 12, 1912, Daisy's dream came true! On this day, Daisy registered the first two troops of girls in Savannah, Georgia. That is why March 12 is the Girl Scout birthday. These first Girl Scouts found out that girls can do all sorts of exciting things. They went on hikes, formed basketball teams, and learned how to camp. These are some of the same things I do with my troop today. How about you?

Girl Scouting became a big hit all over the United States . . . and the world, too! Whenever a leader had a new idea, Daisy would always say, "Have you asked the girls?" Daisy continued to work very hard telling everyone she knew about Girl Scouting. When she died in 1927, there were 168,000 Girl Scouts in the United States. She had a special dream—and she made it come true!

People around the world admire the wonderful work she did. The Juliette Low World Friendship Fund was started to help bring girls from different countries closer together. A ship, a United States postage stamp, and a federal government building were all named for her, and a sculpture of Daisy was placed in the Georgia state capitol. Her home in Savannah, Georgia, is now a national Girl Scout center called the Birthplace.

That's the end of the story that Mrs. Carerras shared with us. Just as I shared her story with you, girls everywhere get to share the special gift that Juliette Gordon Low gave us—Girl Scouts!

More About Girl Scouting

As a Brownie Girl Scout, you may be new to Girl Scouting, or you may have joined as a Daisy Girl Scout. Brownie Girl Scouts are six through eight years old or in the first, second, or third grade.

This handbook is for you to use during your Brownie Girl Scout years. Each chapter has fun activities and stories that will help you learn about Girl Scouting, yourself, family, friends, your community, and the world all around you.

The last chapter has 40 Brownie Girl Scout Try-Its. Try-Its are triangle-shaped patches that Brownie Girl Scouts can get for trying or learning about something new. The chapter "Brownie Girl Scout Try-Its" has lots more information about Try-Its.

Many parts of the book have places for you to write or draw. If you do not have enough space, add another piece of paper to the page. Then, you will have a record of all your Brownie Girl Scout adventures.

You will also see Suzy Safety throughout the book. She is there to remind you to do things in a safe way.

Are you ready to begin your adventures as a Brownie Girl Scout? Let's find out more about Girl Scouting.

> **O**n my honor, I will try:
> To serve God and my country,
> To help people at all times,
> And to live by the Girl Scout Law.

The Girl Scout Promise and Law

All Girl Scouts make the Girl Scout Promise. The words in this Promise are:

These words say a lot about being a Girl Scout.

Let's look at what a Girl Scout says she will do:

On my honor, I will try—This means that a Girl Scout promises to work hard to be her best at all times. The words that follow tell what a Girl Scout will try to do.

To serve God—There are many ways to serve God. Your beliefs are very personal. You may go to a church, a temple, a mosque, a special place indoors or outdoors. You may learn about your beliefs with your family. Every day you try to act in the way that your beliefs and your family teach you.

And my country—A Girl Scout may serve her country in many ways. You can say the Pledge of Allegiance and be in a flag ceremony. You can obey the laws of your community and your country. You can learn more about your country. You can help your family, your neighborhood, and your community. What else can you do?

To help people at all times—A Girl Scout tries to help people. Helping someone carry packages is one small way. There are big ways to help, too. You could teach math to someone younger than you. You can fix something that is broken and you can plant trees to help the environment. What are some other ways to help people?

To live by the Girl Scout Law—The ten parts of the Girl Scout Law are ten ways that you can try to be the best person you can be. Try saying the Girl Scout Law aloud:

I *will do my best:*
To be honest
To be fair
To help where I am needed
To be cheerful
To be friendly and considerate
To be a sister to every Girl Scout
To respect authority
To use resources wisely
To protect and improve the world around me
To show respect for myself and others through my words and actions.

Why not draw or find pictures that show people living by the Girl Scout Law? Your pictures can remind you of what you can do to live by the Girl Scout Law.

The Worlds of Interest

Girl Scouts have five exciting worlds of interest to explore:

The World of Well-Being helps you learn more about how you are special and how to take care of yourself.

The World of People is about others—your family and your friends, people different from yourself, and people around the world.

The World of Today and Tomorrow has opportunities to discover how things work and how things happen, and how you can be ready for the future.

The World of the Arts has puppets and dance, music, pottery, weaving, painting, and much more.

The World of the Out-of-Doors explores the natural world surrounding your home, community, city, or camp.

When you do things in Girl Scouting, you will learn to be the best you can be. You will make new friends and learn about people from all different places, religions, cultures, and races. Girl Scouting will help you learn how to make decisions and decide how to act. You will do service projects that help other people or the community.

The Brownie Story

Brownies have always been known for being honest, fair, and helpful. Have you heard about Brownies? Do you know how Brownie Girl Scouts were named? Here is one version of the story.

ary and Tommy lived with their father and grandmother. Their father worked very hard all day and their grandmother was too old to do the housework.

Their father tried his best to keep the house clean. Mary and Tommy didn't help him very much. They just played all day long.

"Children are hard to care for," said Father.

"Children are a blessing!" said Grandmother.

"Not my children," said Father. "They do not help me a bit."

Just then, Mary and Tommy ran in, their shoes covered with mud.

"Wipe your feet outside!" said Father.

"What makes Father so angry, Granny?" asked Tommy and Mary.

"He is tired and you two do not help him. What this house needs is a brownie or two."

"What is a brownie, Granny?"

"A very helpful little person. She came in before the family was up and did all sorts of chores. The brownie always ran off before anyone could see her, but they could hear her laughing and playing about the house sometimes."

"How nice! Did they pay her, Granny?"

HOO! HOO!
HOO HOO

come. There's plenty of work for her to do here."

So Mary and Tommy put out some cookies and juice, and went off to bed.

That night, Mary could hardly sleep. She kept thinking about the brownie.

"There's an owl living in the old shed by the pond," she thought. "If it is the Wise Old Owl, she can tell me where to find a brownie. When the moon rises, I'll go look for the Wise Old Owl."

The moon rose and Mary hurried to the pond in the woods.

Everything was so still that Mary could hear her heart beating. Then suddenly, "Hoo! Hoo!" said a voice behind her.

"No, brownies always help for love. But the family left her some treats at night like cookies, fruit, and juice. She liked that."

"Oh, Granny, where are the brownies now?"

"Only the Wise Old Owl knows, my dear."

"Who is the Wise Old Owl, Granny?"

"I don't know exactly, my dear."

"Oh, I wish she hadn't gone away!" said Mary and Tommy together. "May we put out some juice and cookies for her? Maybe she will come back if we do."

"Well," said Grandmother, "she's welcome if she chooses to

"It's an owl!" said Mary. "Maybe it's the one I'm looking for."

The owl flew by her onto a beam that ran under the roof of the shed and said, "Come up! Come up!"

The owl could talk! Then it must be the Wise Old Owl! Mary climbed up the beam, and said, "Please, where can I find a brownie to come and live with us?"

"That's it, is it?" said the owl. "Well, I know of two brownies that live in your house."

"In our house!" said Mary. "Then why don't they help us?"

"Perhaps they don't know what has to be done," said the owl.

"Just tell me where to find those brownies," said Mary, "and I'll show them what needs to be done. There is plenty to do at our house!"

"Well, Mary, I can tell you how to find one of the brownies. Go to the pond in the woods when the moon is shining and turn yourself around three times while you say

this charm:

"Twist me and turn me and show me the elf.

I looked in the water and saw _____ ."

Then look into the pond to see the brownie. When you see the brownie, you will think of a word that ends the magic rhyme."

Mary reached the edge of the pond in no time. She slowly turned herself around three times while she said the rhyme:

"Twist me and turn me and show me the elf.

I looked in the water and saw _____ ."

She stopped, looked into the pond, and saw only her own face.

"How silly," said Mary. "There's no word to rhyme with elf, anyway. Belf! Helf! Jelf! Melf! I saw nothing but myself! Myself? That rhymes with elf! How strange! Something must be wrong! I'll go back and ask the Wise Old Owl about it."

Mary went back to the shed and told the Wise Old Owl she saw nothing but herself.

"And what did you expect to see?" asked the owl.

"A brownie," said Mary.

"And what are brownies like?" asked the owl.

"Granny says brownies are very helpful little persons. I saw no one but myself when I looked in the pond and I'm not a brownie."

"All children can be brownies," said the owl. "Couldn't you help out around the house and pick up your own things?"

"I don't think I would like it," Mary said.

"Would you rather be someone who makes work instead of doing it?" asked the owl.

"Oh, no!" cried Mary, "I don't want to be like that. I'll tell Tommy and we'll both try to be brownies."

"That's the way to talk!" said the owl. "Come on, I'll take you home."

Before Mary knew it, she was in her own bed. When daylight came, she woke up Tommy and told him what had happened. Together they crept downstairs and did every bit of work they could find to do before their father woke up. Then they went happily back to bed.

When Father came downstairs, he looked around and rubbed his eyes. The table was set, the floor was clean, and the room was as bright and shiny as a new penny.

At first, Father could not say a word. Then he ran to the foot of the stairs, shouting, "Mother! Tommy! Mary! Our brownie has come back!"

One morning, Father woke up very early and heard laughter coming from the kitchen. "It must be the brownie," he thought. He went downstairs, opened the kitchen door, and saw Mary and Tommy dancing around the room.

"What's this?" he asked.

"It's the brownies! We are the brownies!" sang Tommy and Mary.

"But who did all the work? Where are the real brownies?"

"Here!" said Mary and Tommy as they ran into their father's arms.

When Granny came downstairs, Father told her how he had found the brownies.

"What do you think of it all, Mother?" asked Father.

"Children are a blessing," said Grandmother. "I told you so."

Just like Mary, there are many ways to show how you are a Brownie Girl Scout. Can you think of some? What are some things you'd like to do as a Brownie Girl Scout?

Special Girl Scout Ways

In a **Brownie Girl Scout Ring**, Brownie Girl Scouts get together to make their group decisions. Girls and their Brownie Girl Scout leader plan things to do in troop meetings, camping trips, and service projects.

The **Girl Scout sign** is made when you say the Girl Scout Promise. Hold your right hand like the picture shows you. The three raised fingers stand for the three parts of the Girl Scout Promise.

The **Girl Scout handshake** is the way Girl Scout friends greet each other. Shake hands with your left hand while giving the Girl Scout sign with your right hand.

In a **friendship circle**, stand in a circle and cross your right hand over your left. Hold hands with the people standing next to you.

A **friendship squeeze** is begun by one person in the friendship circle. When you feel your hand squeezed, you do the same to the person next to you. Everyone is silent as the friendship squeeze is passed. It stands for friendship with Girl Scouts everywhere.

The **Girl Scout motto** is "Be prepared." Girl Scouts try to be ready to help when they are needed. They try to be ready for emergencies and be able to take care of themselves.

The **Girl Scout slogan** is "Do a good turn daily." What do you think this means? Even the smallest act can be very helpful.

The **quiet sign** is a way to let everyone know it is time to be quiet. Someone raises her right hand. She keeps her five fingers up to remind others of the fifth part of the Girl Scout Law, "I will do my best to be friendly and considerate." Each person who sees this sign stops talking and raises her hand until everyone is quiet. What are some good reasons to use the quiet sign?

Girl Scout Ceremonies

Girl Scouts hold ceremonies for many reasons. Some ceremonies celebrate a special day in Girl Scouting and others are a way for a group to share their feelings. Girl Scout ceremonies can be short or they can be most of a meeting; they can take place indoors or outdoors.

Your Brownie Girl Scout ceremonies can include Brownie Girl Scouts, other girls in Girl Scouting, Girl Scout leaders, other Girl Scout adults, and special guests like family and friends.

In a ceremony, you can:

• Say the Pledge of Allegiance.

• Honor the flag.
• Say the Girl Scout Promise and Law.
• Light candles or hold flashlights.
• Sing songs.
• Recite poems.
• Read special sayings.
• Tell or act out stories.

In the ceremony opening, everyone learns the reason for the ceremony. The middle is the celebration, and the closing is the time to thank guests and say goodbye.

Songs and music are a special part of Girl Scout ceremonies. The "Brownie Girl Scout Smile Song" is the Brownie Girl Scouts' special song. The words and music are printed on this page. Why not try singing it?

· · · · · · · · · · · · · · · ·
Girl Scouting's Special Days
· · · · · · · · · · · · · · · ·

Do you celebrate some special holidays? Girl Scouts also have some special days.

October 31

Juliette Low's birthday (also known as Founder's Day).

You can honor Juliette Low on her birthday in many different ways:

- Use "The Story of Girl Scouting" to put on a play, skit, or puppet show about Juliette Low's life.
- Invite another troop to celebrate with you and have a party.

Brownie Smile Song

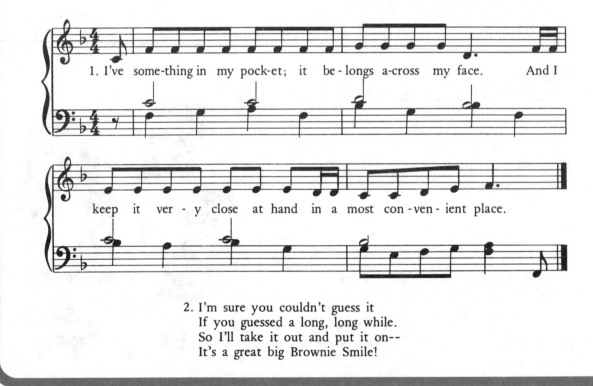

1. I've some-thing in my pock-et; it be-longs a-cross my face. And I

keep it ver-y close at hand in a most con-ven-ient place.

2. I'm sure you couldn't guess it
   If you guessed a long, long while.
   So I'll take it out and put it on--
   It's a great big Brownie Smile!

Used by kind permission of Harriet F. Heywood.

- Give money to the Juliette Low World Friendship Fund. Part of this fund is used to send Girl Scouts to other countries and to bring Girl Guides and Girl Scouts to the United States. The other part is used to help Girl Scouts and Girl Guides around the world.

February 22

Thinking Day is the birthday of both Lord Baden-Powell and Lady Baden-Powell, the World Chief Guide. This is the day that Girl Scouts and Girl Guides everywhere "think about" each other.

They show the spirit of Girl Scouting and Girl Guiding that brings together all members of the World Association of Girl Guides and Girl Scouts in international friendship. To celebrate Thinking Day, you could:

- Invite a Girl Scout who has traveled outside the United States to share her experiences with you.
- Make Thinking Day cards and send them to other Girl Scouts in your area.
- Give to the Juliette Low World Friendship Fund.
- Learn more about people who live in another country.

March 12

This is the day of the Girl Scout birthday, the date in 1912 when the first 18 Girl Scout members were officially registered. The week in which March 12 falls is known as Girl Scout Week. Some girls may celebrate a Girl Scout Sunday or Girl Scout Sabbath. These fall on the weekend before the Girl Scout birthday. You could plan a special day with family and friends and with other Girl Scouts in your neighborhood and community. You might try especially hard to let others know more about Girl Scouting during this week.

April 22

Girl Scout Leader's Day is a special day to honor Girl Scout leaders all over the country. What are some ways you could honor your Girl Scout leader? Could you plan a party, write a poem, sing a song? What could you do with others?

Insignia and Recognitions

The drawings below show you where to put your membership pins, other insignia, and any Try-It patches you may earn.

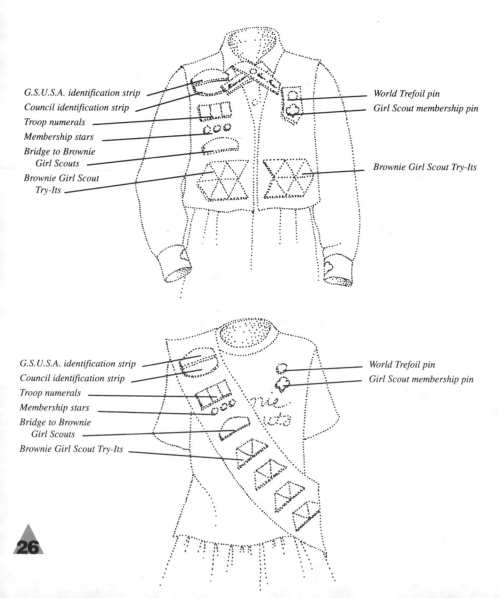

G.S.U.S.A. identification strip
Council identification strip
Troop numerals
Membership stars
Bridge to Brownie Girl Scouts
Brownie Girl Scout Try-Its

World Trefoil pin
Girl Scout membership pin

Brownie Girl Scout Try-Its

G.S.U.S.A. identification strip
Council identification strip
Troop numerals
Membership stars
Bridge to Brownie Girl Scouts
Brownie Girl Scout Try-Its

World Trefoil pin
Girl Scout membership pin

Brownie Girl Scout Uniform

The uniform and its different pieces let other people see that you are a Brownie Girl Scout. The pictures below show different styles of the Brownie Girl Scout uniform.

Brownie Girl Scout Insignia and Recognitions

Girl Scout insignia are the pins and patches that you wear on your uniform that show you are a Girl Scout. Try-Its are recognitions you can earn as a Brownie Girl Scout.

Many religious groups have their own recognitions for girls of their faith who are Girl Scouts. If you are interested in the religious recognitions, you can find out about them from your Girl Scout leader or your religious group.

The **Brownie Girl Scout pin** tells others that you are a Brownie Girl Scout. It is shaped like a trefoil, which means three leaves. The leaves stand for the three parts of the Girl Scout Promise. In the middle of the pin is a brownie. You may wear your Brownie Girl Scout pin even when you are not wearing your uniform.

The **World Trefoil pin** shows that you are part of the World Association of Girl Guides and Girl Scouts. The three leaves represent the Girl Scout Promise. The flame stands for loving all the people in the world. The compass needle is to guide you, and the two stars are the Girl Scout Promise and Law. The outer circle is for the Worldwide Association of Girl Guides and Girl Scouts, and the golden yellow trefoil on a bright blue background stands for the sun shining over the children of the world. You may wear it on your regular clothes as well as on your uniform.

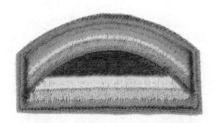

The **Bridge to Brownie Girl Scouts patch** is for girls who were once Daisy Girl Scouts and did special activities before becoming Brownie Girl Scouts.

The **Girl Scouts U.S.A. strip** shows that you are part of the family of Girl Scouts in the United States of America.

The **Girl Scout council strip** shows the name of your local Girl Scout council. Every Girl Scout **troop** has its own **number**. The number is given to your troop by your Girl Scout council.

The **membership star** stands for one year of membership in Girl Scouting. You get a star for each year you are a Girl Scout. The color of the circle behind the star tells the age level. The color green shows that you got the star as a Brownie Girl Scout, and a blue disc shows that you were once a Daisy Girl Scout.

Brownie Girl Scout Try-Its are patches, or recognitions, that show you have tried learning how to do many new things. You get a patch for each set of activities that you have tried.

Girl Scout Age Levels

All girls in kindergarten through the twelfth grade or five through 17 years of age can be members of Girl Scouting in the United States. Girl Scouting is for girls of all religions and traditions, of all races, and of all cultures. Girl Scouts of all ages in the United States do make the Girl Scout Promise and accept the Girl Scout Law, just like you.

The five age levels in Girl Scouting are:

- Daisy Girl Scouts—ages 5–6 or grades K, 1
- Brownie Girl Scouts—ages 6, 7, 8 or grades 1, 2, 3
- Junior Girl Scouts—ages 8, 9, 10, 11 or grades 3, 4, 5, 6
- Cadette Girl Scouts—ages 11, 12, 13, 14 or grades 6, 7, 8, 9
- Senior Girl Scouts—ages 14, 15, 16, 17 or grades 9, 10, 11, 12

Daisy
Girl Scout

Brownie
Girl Scout

Junior
Girl Scout

Cadette
Girl Scout

Senior
Girl Scout

Investiture or Rededication

After you have learned the Girl Scout Promise and Law, you are ready to be invested. An investiture is a special ceremony in which you officially become a Girl Scout. As part of the ceremony, you make the Girl Scout Promise. If you were a Daisy Girl Scout, you have already been invested and you will be rededicated as a Brownie Girl Scout.

Investiture and rededication are important ceremonies in Girl Scouting. If you are being invested, you will receive your Brownie Girl Scout pin. If you are being rededicated, you will repeat the Girl Scout Promise and Law.

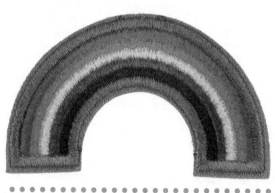

Bridging

Moving from one age level to another is called bridging. You will "cross the bridge" from Brownie to Junior Girl Scouting, the next age level, at the end of your last year as a Brownie Girl Scout.

Girl Scout National Centers

Girl Scouts from everywhere in the United States can meet other Girl Scouts at two special places called "national centers."

The Juliette Gordon Low Girl Scout National Center, also known as "The Birthplace," is the home in Savannah, Georgia, where Juliette Low was born. People can visit this historic house museum and program center and learn about Juliette Low's life. Girl Scout troops can take part in many fun activities.

Edith Macy Conference Center is near New York City in Briarcliff Manor, New York. Adults learn more about Girl Scouting there.

Edith Macy Conference Center

Juliette Gordon Low Girl Scout National Center

World Centers

Our Cabaña (Mexico), Our Chalet (Switzerland), Pax Lodge (England), and Sangam (India) are four centers where older Girl Guides and Girl Scouts from all over the world can meet to get to know each other and share ideas, attend events, work on service projects, or learn something new.

Brownie Girl Scout Scavenger Hunt!

Leyla is new to Brownie Girl Scouting. Help her find in this book each of the items listed below. Circle each item you find. Look back through the chapter if you need help!

Girl Scout sign
Girl Scout handshake
Friendship circle
Girl Scout Promise
Girl Scout slogan
Daisy Girl Scout
Brownie Girl Scout Ring
World Trefoil pin
Brownie Girl Scout pin
Brownie Girl Scout Try-Its
Brownie Girl Scout Handbook
Girl Scout birthday
Membership star and disc
Junior Girl Scout
Girl Scout motto
Suzy Safety

Taking Care of Yourself and Your Home

Marisol stretched her legs as long as they could reach and pointed her toes under the bed covers. She had danced across the stage, the star of the Ballet Folklórico. Everyone was standing and clapping and throwing red roses, until this B-Z-Z noise got louder and louder and louder. She was dreaming! The B-Z-Z noise was the alarm clock! "6:30 A.M." Across the room, she could see the curled-up shape of her sister, Lisa, pillow over her head. "I'm always the one to get up first," Marisol thought. "And I have to make sure Lisa gets dressed, and make breakfast for both of us, and

Marisol Starts a Club

find her missing homework. I'm the responsible one. I'm the oldest." She looked at the alarm clock—6:35. If she didn't have to get Lisa ready, she could sleep until 7:00—and dream some more about dancing. . . .

"Lisa, get up, get in the bathroom." Marisol pulled the pillow away from her sister's head.

"Oh, Marisol, please, five more minutes," Lisa begged.

"Not one more second! You have to get up now." Marisol watched her leave the room. "Every morning she asks for five more minutes. I don't have five extra minutes."

Marisol quickly made both beds. She chose her outfit—sneakers, jeans skirt, pink T-shirt, and an outfit for Lisa. She walked quietly down the hall. She knew her dad would be sleeping. He didn't get home from work until midnight.

She put two waffles in the microwave, poured some juice and some milk. She measured the coffee into the basket and started the coffee

maker. Her mom got home at 7:30 A.M. She worked the night shift at the hospital and was very happy to sit for a moment and have a cup of coffee when she got home.

Her mom had started working again last month. Her mom had talked with Marisol about doing more at home, especially in the mornings and after school. Marisol wanted her mom to be proud of her, but sometimes she wished she could be the younger one or her mom wouldn't go to work at all.

Lisa's homework was under the dog's bed. Lisa's sneaker wouldn't stay tied. Lisa couldn't find her lunch. Marisol found it in the bathroom. "Why did you bring your lunch to the bathroom?" Marisol looked at her sister and said, "Forget it, let's go." And she made sure she locked the door behind her as they left.

At lunch, Marisol sat with her very closest friends—Raza, Tamara, and Carol. She opened her lunch bag. "Oh, no, I have Lisa's lunch. She won't eat anything but peanut

butter and I hate peanut butter. Little sisters are such a pain!"

Raza looked up from her tuna fish and said, "Have half of my sandwich. I wish I had a little sister. Older brothers can be a pain, too."

"But, you don't have to be responsible," and Marisol told them all the things she did every day.

"Since my parents got divorced,

I do lots of things at home," Tamara said. "My Mom and I painted all the rooms in the house. I helped her put down tiles in the kitchen. I even help her take care of the car. She said if we can't keep it running, we'd be in big trouble. New cars are too expensive!"

Raza added, "My mom has always worked and lots of times she gets home late, so she makes a bunch of meals on the weekend and when she's going to be late, I get dinner ready. I never even think about it. I just do it."

Carol said, "I have two little brothers *and* a little sister. My mom always asks me to help her look after them. She says she doesn't know what she'd do without me. And I always feel good when she says that."

Marisol thought about all the times her mom told her what a big help she was. She thought about how good she felt when she made the coffee for her mom in the morning. "I feel really good, too, when I

do things around the house," Marisol said. "We're all very responsible. I have a great idea. Let's form a club—The Responsible Ones. We can call ourselves The ROS, for short. We can take care of ourselves and take care of our home and help our fam-

ilies and help each other—what do you think?"

Of course, it was such a good idea that Carol and Tamara and Raza agreed on the spot and their club, The Responsible Ones, was started that same day.

What responsibilities do you have? You probably have some responsibilities to take care of yourself. You need to keep yourself safe and take care of your body and your clothing. You need to eat food that is good for you and you need to feel good about yourself. Do you have responsibilities at home? Do you take care of your room? Do you do other things inside and outside your home? In this chapter, you will have fun learning about taking care of yourself and your home.

Taking Care of Yourself

You only have one very special body. Being good to yourself now will help you as you grow up.

Your Body Is One of a Kind

No one has a body just like yours. Bodies come in all shapes and all sizes. You have your own eye and hair color, hair texture, and skin color. Maybe you have freckles. Maybe you are tall. Maybe you are short. There is no one best body. How are bodies different? Try these four activities and find out.

1. Tape pieces of newspaper together to form a large sheet. Lie down on your back on it. Ask a buddy to take a crayon or marker and trace the shape of your body onto the paper. Draw in your face and clothing to complete this picture of you.

2. Try "Tracing Your Shadow" in the Me and My Shadow Brownie Girl Scout Try-It. Compare your silhouette with the others in your troop/group.

3. You could compare your body measurements with those of other people. You could also compare the measurements of different parts of your own body. Are different parts of your body the same length? Are the distances around parts of your body the same as the different lengths?

Get some ribbons, long strips of newspaper, or tape measures. Measure different parts of your body. Make a strip or ribbon for each of these:

- The distance around your neck
- The distance around your wrist
- The distance around your head
- The distance around your ankle

Which is bigger? Now measure the distance between your elbow and the tip of your longest finger. Measure the distance between your knee and the bottom of your foot. Which is longer?

4. Everyone has different fingerprints. Find out what yours look like. On a piece of paper, with a soft, dark pencil, make a spot about the size of a quarter. Press one finger at a time on the spot and then press your fingers in the outline here. You can put clear tape over your fingerprints to keep them from getting messed up.

Compare your fingerprints with other Brownie Girl Scouts in your group or with your family. What did you discover?

No one in the entire world has the same fingerprints as you. Scientists can identify people by their fingerprints. They can look at a set of fingerprints and find out whose they are. Scientists use computers to compare a person's fingerprints with the fingerprints they have in a computer file. Knowing someone's name through her fingerprints can help scientists find someone who is missing or find someone who has broken the law. Can you think of other uses for fingerprints?

Caring for Your Body

What do you do in the morning when you first get up to care for your body? What do you do at night before you go to bed? People care for their bodies in different ways. Some people need to wash their hair every day and some only once a week. You might need to start using powder or a deodorant or you might not need to use a deodorant until you are much older. You might have oily skin that you wash often or you might have dry skin that you moisturize with cream or lotion. Maybe your skin is becoming oilier only in certain spots. You might want to use powder on your feet or in your sneakers or on your body when you know that you will sweat a lot. When you wash your hands and feet, take some extra time to make sure your nails are clean.

Changes in Your Body

These body care tips are important for your entire life. As you grow older, you will notice that your body changes. Parts of your body grow at different rates. You might notice that your nose looks bigger or your feet have grown. As you grow older, you may notice changes in your body that make you look more adult. These changes are called puberty and may start in some girls when they are eight, nine, or ten years old. Other girls may not have these changes until they are 16 or 17. Remember, every body is different! It is important to talk to a family member or adult you know and trust about these changes. Remember, change is a normal part of being a human being!

Try making a time line that shows how you have grown over the years. Here are some suggestions for your time line. What other things can you include?

My Time Line

Years   0   1   2   3   4   5   6   7   8   9   10

- When you lost your first tooth
- When you had your first birthday party
- When you said your first word
- When you went to school for the first time

Basics of Body Care for Now and Later

Here is a list of the basic ways to take care of yourself. Follow these and you will look good and feel your best now and into the future.

- Exercise.
- Eat a variety of nutritious foods.
- Get a good night's sleep.
- Dress properly for the weather.
- See your doctor and your dentist for regular checkups.
- Learn to do things safely.
- Keep your body and clothing clean.

Eating Right

Think of all the different kinds of foods you eat. Some foods may taste better to you than others. You might like some foods that are good for you. You might also like some foods that are not so good for you. Your body needs lots of different kinds of foods to stay healthy and your body needs the right kinds of foods. The food pyramid is one way of looking at everything you eat to make sure you eat the right food in the right amount.

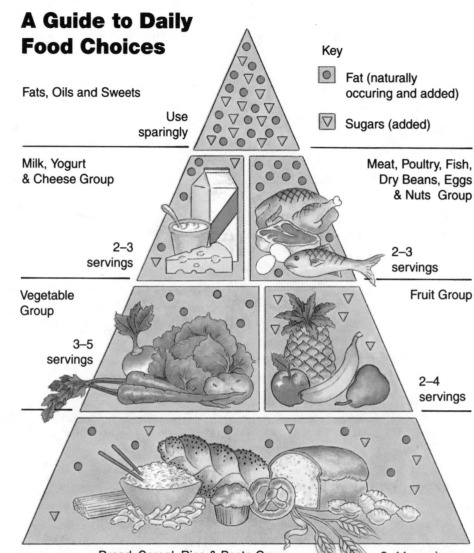

A Guide to Daily Food Choices

Key

Fat (naturally occuring and added)

Sugars (added)

Fats, Oils and Sweets — Use sparingly

Milk, Yogurt & Cheese Group — 2–3 servings

Meat, Poultry, Fish, Dry Beans, Eggs & Nuts Group — 2–3 servings

Vegetable Group — 3–5 servings

Fruit Group — 2–4 servings

Bread, Cereal, Rice & Pasta Group — 6–11 servings

Can you think of the names of some foods that are good for you in each of the categories? Check the food pyramid for help.

Milk, Yogurt, and Cheese Group

_____

_____

_____

Bread, Cereal, Rice, and Pasta Group

_____

_____

_____

Vegetable Group

_____

_____

Meat, Poultry, Fish, Dry Beans, Eggs, and Nuts Group

_____

_____

_____

Fats, Oils, and Sweets Group

_____

_____

_____

MENU

Breakfast

_____

_____

_____

Dinner

_____

_____

_____

Lunch

_____

_____

_____

Snack

_____

_____

When you are being good to your body, you are giving it nutrients—what it needs to grow healthy and strong. Fresh fruits, vegetables, whole wheat and grains, beans, and milk have lots of nutrients. Potato chips, candy, sodas, and cake are not good for your body. They don't help your body grow. You could gain too much weight or you could have problems with your heart. You need fruits and vegetables, a small amount of meat or other protein, milk or yogurt or cheese (low-fat is better), breads, cereals, rice and pasta (spaghetti and macaroni), lots of water—and just a little fat in your diet.

Think about the foods you eat each day. Are you eating healthy foods? Are you eating the right amounts? Think of what you can do to eat healthfully. Can you make a one-day menu (breakfast, lunch, dinner, and one snack) that follows the kinds of foods and amounts of foods from the food pyramid? Compare menus with those of other girls in your troop and group. You can see that there are many different ways to eat healthy foods.

Carrot, celery, or other raw vegetable sticks

Raisins

Fruit-juice popsicles

Fresh fruit mixed with low-fat cottage cheese or plain low-fat yogurt

Sliced bananas rolled in chopped nuts

Can you think of some healthy snacks? Make a list. A few are already written for you.

Try making this Food Pyramid Party Mix. You will need:

- 1/4 cup peanut butter or chocolate chips
- 1/2 cup dried banana or apple chips
- 1/4 cup sunflower seeds
- 1/2 cup raisins
- 1/2 cup air-popped popcorn
- 2/3 cup low-salt, low-sugar granola cereal
- 1/3 cup dry roasted peanuts

Mix well in a serving bowl. Serves three people, about one cup each. How much of each ingredient do you need to serve six people? twelve people? the people in your Girl Scout troop or group?

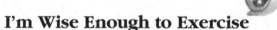

move every day. Here are some fun ways to move.

- Try the "Animal Moves" activity in the Dancercize Try-It.

- Pick some of your favorite music and make up some dance movements to it.

- Play follow-the-leader using as many different movements as possible.

- Invent your own exercise routine. Remember, exercise shouldn't hurt, so start slowly.

- Take a walk to music. Pick a music tape that has a fast beat, put it in a small portable cassette player with headphones, and try walking to it. Use different songs to start slowly and end slowly. Make more than one tape of different kinds of music and share them

with your family and friends.

- Form an exercise club. Plan on meeting at least three times a week. Take turns leading the exercises.

Caring for Your Clothes and Home

Taking Care of Your Clothes

It is important for your body to be clean and healthy. It is important to eat right and exercise. It is also important for your clothes to be clean. Imagine how your clean skin feels if you put dirty clothes on it? Think of your nice clean toes . . . in dirty smelly socks? Ugh! Keeping your clothing clean and neat is easy. Look at the pictures. The pictures will help you learn how to take care of your clothing. You can also ask an adult to help you learn:

- How to sew on buttons and make simple repairs.
- How to hand-wash clothing in a sink or basin.

I'm Wise Enough to Exercise

Fitness is important. You can eat good food, but you also have to move your body to keep it strong. Many of the active games you like to play are good exercise. Swimming, running, skating, walking, bicycling, dancing, and jumping rope are all good ways to keep fit. Sitting in front of a television set won't even exercise your eyes! You need to

- How to operate a washing machine.
- How to sort clothing to be washed. Learn which temperature of water to use and which colors are washed together.
- How to use and store an iron.
- How to arrange clothes neatly in closets and drawers.

It saves lots of time in the morning if you spend a little bit of time the night before choosing the clothes you will wear to school. Then, fold them neatly or put them together on a hanger so you can get dressed quickly in the morning.

What are some of your favorite outfits to wear to school? (If you wear a uniform to school, think of your favorite outfits for the weekend.) What tops (blouses and shirts) and bottoms (skirts and pants) look good together? Can you mix and match to make some more outfits?

Write some of your favorite outfits here.

Dressing for the Weather

What do you do if it is raining outside? If it is windy? If it is very sunny? How do you know what the weather will be like?

In some places, you can call to find out the kind of weather you will have that day. How else can you find out?

With permission, call the weather number in your area or look in a newspaper or listen to the weather report on the radio or on television.

Four types of weather are shown on these two pages. Draw pictures of the types of clothes you need for each, or cut out pictures from magazines or catalogs (get permission first) and paste them in the spaces at right.

Taking Care of Your Home

There are a number of things you should know how to do around your home. Ask an adult to show you:

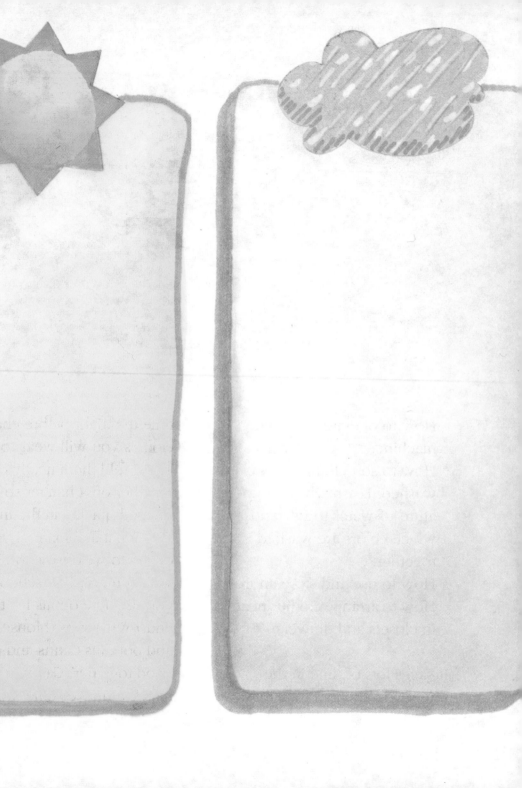

- How to put fresh batteries in a flashlight.
- How to program a VCR and how to clean it.
- How to install a water-saver shower head.
- What to do if you smell gas. Turn off any flames, open windows and doors, and leave immediately. Do not touch a light switch or pick up the telephone. Electricity can make a spark and cause an explosion. Never light a match! Call the gas company or fire department from a phone outside.
- How to warm up food for dinner in the microwave or on the stove or in the oven. Learn the right dishes to use, the right way to handle hot dishes, and the correct temperature and time to heat the food.

Learn what to do when the power goes out. Does your family

inside for a day and a freezer for two days if it is not opened a lot. Fill the bathtub with water and fill some pots with water, too. Sometimes in a big storm when the power goes out, the water from your tap can become bad to drink. You will hear on the radio if this has happened.

keep an emergency supply of candles, small cans of cooking fuel or a camp stove, batteries, and a portable radio? Unplug or turn off all appliances. When the power comes back on, a big surge of power can break them. Keep the refrigerator door closed. Keep your freezer door closed. A refrigerator can stay cold

Learn:

- How to put new rubber washer blades on a car windshield.
- How to check that the car has enough window washer fluid.
- How to use a vacuum cleaner.
- How to sort trash for things that can be recycled.
- How to make a bed.
- How to fix a chair or table that shakes or wobbles.
- How to clean the bathtub, sink, and toilet.
- How to repot a plant.
- How to unclog a drain.
- How to test a smoke alarm.
- How to plug and unplug a phone.
- How to use an extension cord properly.

Demonstrate some of these for your troop or group or friends and family. Try showing the others how to do these without using any words. Can they guess what you are doing?

Home Repairs

You need to learn how to use tools properly to take good care of your home. Some tools are simple. You can use them to make easy repairs. Have an adult show you how to use these tools:

- Hammer
- Common screwdriver
- Phillips screwdriver
- Sandpaper
- Pliers
- Wrench
- Level
- Tape measure

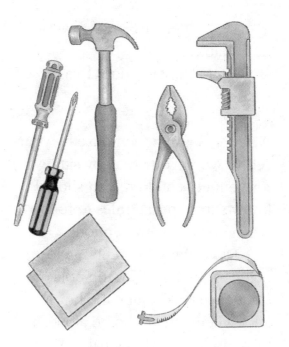

Now practice using these tools yourself. (Ask your family first.) Make sure you follow these rules:

- An adult is with you.
- You have space to work.
- The tools are in good condition.
- Use the right tool for the job.

Here are some examples of repairs you can make:

- Using sandpaper to smooth wood that has splinters.
- Hammering a nail in the wall to hang a picture.
- Tightening screws or bolts that have become loose.

Board Tic Tac Toe is a game you can make using simple tools. Make it for yourself or to give as a gift. You need:

- One square flat board
- 9 1″ nails
- 5 large buttons of the same color
- 5 large buttons of a different color
- A ruler
- A pencil
- An ink marker
- A sheet of sandpaper
- A hammer
- 10 twist ties for closing plastic bags

Follow this diagram to make your board. Do the following:

1. Have someone help you make the board 12″ wide and 12″ long.

2. Draw lines like those in the drawing.

3. Hammer a nail in the top part of each box.

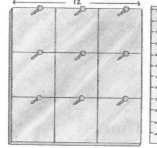

4. Poke a twist tie through each button.

5. You are now ready to play.

6. Each person gets five buttons of the same color. Take turns hanging buttons on the nails instead of writing Xs and Os. The first one to get three of her color in a row wins. Take the buttons down and start again.

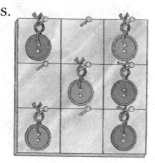

Staying Safe

You can take good care of your body by eating the right foods and by exercising. You can take care of your home and take care of your clothing. But, there is another very important way to take care of yourself—*staying safe*.

Safety Do's and Don'ts

Here are some Do's and Dont's. If a stranger approaches you,

DON'T go near his or her car, even if the person says your mother said it is okay. Get away!

DON'T even get in a conversation. Send him or her to the nearest adult.

DON'T believe any message he or she gives you.

DON'T take any candy, gum, or gifts.

DON'T enter any rooms, elevators, empty streets, or buildings with strangers.

If someone makes you feel funny or if you think someone will hurt you,

DO RUN FOR HELP. Drop everything and run quickly.

DO SHOUT FOR HELP.

When Walking:

DO walk with a friend.

DON'T take shortcuts through dark alleys, deserted buildings, or parks.

At Home:

DO hang up if someone you don't know asks you questions on the phone, even if he or she sounds very friendly.

DON'T tell anyone that you are home alone.

DON'T open a door to a stranger.

When you are in the house by yourself or when you are baby sitting for younger children, you should know some special rules to follow when you answer the phone.

DO call your parents, a close neighbor you trust, or the police if someone starts calling the house a lot when you are home alone. Tell them about the phone calls. Ask for someone to stay with you until the adults are home.

DO call the emergency number if you feel frightened or suspicious.

DON'T tell the caller that you are in the house by yourself. If he or she asks for your mom or dad or other adult, just tell the caller that your mom or dad cannot come to the phone right now.

DON'T give out any information. Just ask for the name and phone number and say that someone will return the call. Some homes have Caller ID service and you can see the phone number of the person calling you. Tell the person you have the number and have written it down. Ask for the name and say that someone will call back later. Be polite and then hang up.

In parks and play areas,

DO play where you can be seen by the person taking care of you.

DON'T play in deserted, out-of-the way places, such as abandoned buildings, empty laundry rooms, storerooms, or rooftops.

DON'T leave school grounds during breaks or recess.

DON'T play around construction sites, mining sites, train yards, or any place with large trucks.

When you use public transportation,

DO wait at a busy, well-lighted transit stop.

DO run for help if you see someone you think is dangerous.

DO sit near the conductor or driver.

DO ask the conductor or driver for help if you are worried.

DO change seats if someone near you is making you worried.

When using public restrooms,

DO take someone you know with you.

DON'T talk to strangers or let them near you.

If you see something suspicious or a stranger approaches you, try to remember the following and tell an adult!

- What happened?
- Where did it happen?
- When did it happen?
- What did the person look like? How big was the person? Was he or she old or young, man or woman, boy or girl?

new or old? Was it scratched or dented? Can you remember the license plate number? How many people were in the car?

Safety with People You Know

Lots of people touch you. Parents hug you. Your brothers and sisters touch you when you play. Your baby sitter helps you get ready for bed. Doctors and dentists touch you when you go for a checkup. Some touches are "good" touches. Adults and older children touch your body in ways that do not hurt you or make you feel uncomfortable. Some touches are "bad" touches. If someone's touch makes you feel uneasy or scared, you can say "No!" Practice saying "No!" You can say "No" to adults, even someone you know very well. You can protect

What were the person's hair color, eye color, skin color? Did the person wear glasses? A real or fake mustache? What kinds of clothing did the person wear? Did the person have any special marks or scars that you can remember?

• If the person was in a car, what did the car look like? Did the license plate look different? Did the car look

your body, especially the parts that are covered by a bathing suit. You can say "No" to any touch that makes you feel funny or uncomfortable. You can tell a parent, an adult you trust, a teacher, or a doctor, if you have been touched in a way that feels wrong. It is very important to tell someone.

Practice what you would say in these situations:

- A person you know won't stop tickling you and you don't like it at all.
- Your older brother pinches you very hard.
- A woman comes up to you on the playground and asks if you will show her the way to the closest grocery store.
- A neighbor invites you inside and offers you some cookies. The neighbor says or does something that makes you feel very strange.
- You are home alone and the phone rings. A man asks to speak to your father.
- You are separated from your mother at the shopping mall and a woman you don't know offers to help you find her.

Make a Safety List

You have already learned some safety rules. What does it mean to be safe? You are safe when there is nothing to harm you. What are some things that can harm you? Can you add to this list?

Fire _____

Drunk drivers _____

Poisons _____

_____

_____

_____

_____

_____

_____

_____

_____

_____

_____

_____

_____

What can you do to stay safe?

Emergency Who's Who

You can be ready for emergencies. Ask a family member to help you make a list of numbers to keep by the telephone.

Family Work Numbers _____

_____

Neighbor _____

Fire Department _____

Police _____

Ambulance _____

Health Department _____

Poison Control Center _____

Doctor _____

Dentist _____

What would you say or do if you had to make an emergency call? Follow the emergency guide below.

1. Use the emergency who's who list and dial the number you need.

2. Tell who you are. "Hello, my name is _____ ."

3. Tell where you are. "I am at _____ " (street, apartment, house number, city, state or name of park, trail, building, etc.).

4. Tell what the emergency is. "This is an emergency. I need _____ ."

Stay calm and follow directions.

Think of some emergencies and practice making pretend phone calls. One person can be the police or the emergency operator and another person can make the phone call.

On Your Own at Home

Sometimes you may be at home alone. You may be responsible for your younger sisters and brothers. On page 48 in this book are some basic skills that you should have when you stay alone. Know how to make emergency calls, what to do if there is a fire or if the lights go out, and how to answer the phone. These are good to know all the time, but especially when you are home alone. What can you do when you are by yourself?

Draw a map of your home in the space. Mark the emergency exits, the place where light bulbs and flashlights are kept,  and the place where your family keeps its first-aid supplies.

Talk about the rules your family has made for the times when you are home alone. How do these rules help you stay safe?

Pretend that you are home by yourself. With your Girl Scout troop or group, or your friends and family, practice some  things that can happen when you are by yourself and what you should do.

If you have a micro-wave oven at your Girl Scout meeting place, practice making some  snacks in the microwave. Learn how to use a microwave safely. Learn how to make some snacks that don't need cooking.

Other things to do when you are by yourself:

- First, finish your homework and do any housework or chores you have.
- Try dancing. Dancing is a good way to spend the time. It is healthy and fun.
- Read a book. Visit the library so you have a supply of books to read when you are alone. Reading a favorite book again is also fun.
- Try making your own book. Write or draw a story. You can choose an autobiography, a mystery, a fairy tale, or a cartoon.
- List all the good things about being a girl. There are lots!
- Try a new hairstyle or different combinations of clothing.
- Make puppets. See page 248 for some ideas. Create your own play. Act out some real things that have happened to you.

- Write your name on a piece of paper. See how many new words you can make from the letters in your name.

- Write a letter to someone. Everybody loves to get letters.
- Make a greeting card to thank someone for doing something special or for being a special person to you.
- Try making up your own song. If you have a tape recorder, record your song. Or, try singing along to some of your favorite songs or try

listening to a radio station that plays a type of music different from the music you usually listen to.

Fire Safety

With your family and your Girl Scout group, prepare a plan for what to do in case of fire. In your home, the first part of your plan should be to make your home as safe as possible. Most fires can be prevented. Look for fire hazards. A fire hazard is anything that can cause a fire indoors or outdoors. Make a list of things to do to reduce the danger of fire. The second part should be a home fire drill. Know the best way to get out of your home, especially from the bedrooms. Plan a second way to get out of the house if the first way is blocked by the fire.

Smoke detectors can help make your home safe. Find out about smoke detectors. Does your home have one? How do you check that it is working?

Remember these three words: *stop, drop, roll.*

Look at the picture above. Circle all the fire dangers.

What do you do if your clothes catch on fire?

1. *Stop.* Do not run or walk or jump around. Moving gives more oxygen to the fire and keeps it going.

2. *Drop.* Drop to the ground or floor. Cover your face with your hands.

3. *Roll.* Smother the fire by rolling over slowly.

What would you do if another person's clothes caught on fire?

1. Get the person to the ground.

2. Roll her over or use a coat or blanket to smother the flames.

3. Be careful that your own clothing or hair does not catch on fire.

Sports Safety

Sports are good for your body and your mind. Sports can help your body to be in good shape and can help your mind relax. If you start playing a sport now, you can discover a good way to spend your free time now and when you are older. Try some different sports. You might not like the first sport you try. Maybe you need to play it some more and get a little better at it, before you really enjoy it. Maybe there are some sports you just won't like. That's okay. You will usually find a sport that you like if you try a few. If you want to enjoy sports without having problems, you need to know some safety rules. Take this sports safety quiz. Check your answers. Are you a sports safety winner or loser?

True or False?

1. You should ride your bicycle against the traffic so you can see the cars coming toward you.

2. You should always wear a bicycle helmet when on a bike.

3. In a group of bicycle riders, always cycle in pairs.

4. Wear bright-colored clothing when bicycling at night.

5. If you skate outdoors, you need to wear a helmet, gloves, and knee protectors.

6. If you fall while skating at a rink, ask your "buddy" to help you get up.

7. It is never safe to ice-skate on a pond or lake alone.

8. Warm-up and cool-down exercises should be done when playing sports.

9. It is safe to swim without a lifeguard.

10. Sneakers are the best shoes for horseback riding.

11. Skiers only need sunglasses/goggles on sunny days.

12. Sandals are good shoes for soccer.

13. A street is a good place to jump rope because you have lots of room for the rope to turn.

Check Your Answers

1. False. You should always ride your bicycle in the same direction the traffic is going.

2. True.

3. False. Always cycle in a single file.

4. False. Wear bright-colored clothing when bicycling during the day. Wear light or reflective clothing at night. Make sure you have reflector tape on your bicycle fenders, handlebars, and helmet. Make sure your bike has a light that works.

5. True.

6. False. You should get up quickly on your own. If you use another person to help you, you can easily make her fall.

7. True.

8. True.

9. False. Always swim when a lifeguard is on duty.

10. False. You need boots or shoes with one-inch heels.

11. False. When skiing, you need sunglasses/goggles all the time to protect your eyes.

12. False. You should wear special shoes and shin guards.

13. False. You should play where no cars can hurt you.

Check Your Answers

12–13 right answers—congratulations! You're a safety winner!

9–11 right answers—You're on the first string of the safety team!

5–8 right answers—You're on the second string. Learn some more about safety.

4 and below—Practice, practice, practice! Find out lots more about safety and sports. You'll play better, feel better, and stay safe!

First Aid

First aid is the first help an injured or sick person receives. First aid may be washing a cut, saying things to keep someone calm, or getting a doctor.

You should have a first-aid kit in your home, in your family's car, and on Girl Scout outings.

Here are some things to put in the kit:

- First-aid book
- Soap
- Safety pins
- Scissors
- Tweezers
- Sewing needle
- Matches
- Adhesive tape and sterile gauze dressings
- Clean cloth
- Calamine lotion
- Anti-bacterial antiseptic
- Emergency telephone numbers
- Money for phone calls
- Rubber or plastic gloves
- Simple face mask
- Plastic bag

Infections

A simple cut can be very dangerous if it gets infected. An infection is bacteria growing in your body. This can happen if a cut is not taken care of properly. Signs of infection include swelling, redness, a hot feeling, pain, tenderness, fever, and pus.

If you get a cut, wash your hands with soap and water before cleaning the cut. Seek medical care right away. If you must help someone who has a cut, wear rubber or plastic gloves from your first-aid kit.

Bites and Stings

All bites need first aid because there are lots of bacteria in the mouth. Even small bites can be dangerous. Animal bites can be very bad because some animals carry rabies, a very dangerous disease. Never go near a wild animal or other animal you do not

know. Do not go near an animal you do know if it is acting strangely. People bites can also be bad. People have germs in their mouths, sometimes more than dogs do! If you have been bitten, tell an adult immediately. If you know where the animal is, point it out to an adult. If the animal has run away, describe it to an adult.

If no one is nearby and you get bitten, you might have to give yourself first aid.

1. Wash your hands with soap and water.

2. Wash the wound with soap and water.

3. Rinse the wound well with clear water.

4. Blot the wound dry with a clean towel.

5. Apply a bandage.

6. See a doctor.

If you have to help someone who has been bitten, make sure you wear plastic or rubber gloves from your first-aid kit.

Most insect bites, like mosquito bites, are not serious. Your skin may get itchy and swell up, but the bite soon goes away—especially if you do not scratch it! A bee sting can hurt, but usually it is not dangerous. If you get stung by a bee and the stinger is in your skin, try to scrape the stinger out with a clean fingernail or needle. Don't squeeze the stinger. Press a cold washcloth or an ice cube on the sting.

Some people are very allergic to bees and other insects. If they get stung, they may have a hard time breathing. If someone who is allergic gets stung, she must see a doctor or get to a hospital right away.

Burns

A burn is an injury to your skin from heat or chemicals.

If you have a burn, run cool water, not ice water, over the burned area. Be gentle with your skin and don't break any blisters (the bubbles of skin) that pop up. Put clean cloth bandages over the burned part. Don't put butter or anything greasy on it! Find an adult to help you take care of the burn and to help you decide whether you need to see a doctor or go to a hospital.

Too Much Body Heat

Your body can get too hot. Doctors call this heat exhaustion or heatstroke. You can get sick from the heat if you stay in the heat or in the bright sun too long. Heatstroke

can give you a fever and red, hot skin. It can also make you feel faint or dizzy. An adult should help you cool off by wiping your skin with cool water, putting cold packs on your skin, helping you sit in cool water, and/or finding an air-conditioned place to lie down. Get medical help. Heatstroke is very serious and needs to be treated right away.

The signs of heat exhaustion are feeling weak or feeling like you

might throw up, feeling dizzy, having bad cramps in your stomach, fainting, and having skin that feels cool or cold and wet. Get out of the sun right away and tell an adult that you don't feel well. Put a cool cloth on your forehead and body. Take some sips of water. Lie down and raise your feet. If you don't feel better in an hour, see a doctor.

Too Little Body Heat

Your body can get too cold. This is called hypothermia. If you stay outside too long in cold or windy weather, or when it is wet outside, even on a day that's not so

cold, you can get hypothermia. Wearing the right clothes and a hat is very important. Hypothermia can make you shiver, your teeth chatter, your hands and feet feel cold. You need to get inside right away and slowly eat or drink something that is warm.

Frostbite

When it is very cold, the parts of your body that are not protected can actually freeze. This is called frostbite. Most frostbite happens in fingers, toes, nose, cheeks, and ears. The skin may be slightly red and then turn white or grayish-yellow. There is no pain in the frost-bitten part. You can get blisters and your skin feels cold and numb. Frostbite is dangerous. Go indoors and warm up. Don't rub the skin. Put the part in warm water between 102°F (39°C) and 105°F (41°C) or gently wrap it with a sheet and warm blankets. Find an adult to help. See a doctor right away.

Nosebleeds

Nosebleeds can happen when the air is very dry, if you have had a cold, if you have had too much exercise, if you are in a very high place, like the mountains, or if you hurt your nose. Try to stop the bleeding by sitting down and squeezing your nose firmly for about ten minutes. Placing cold towels on your nose may help. If the bleeding continues, get an adult to help you.

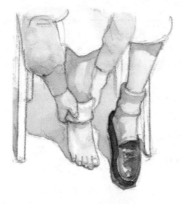

Bumps and Bruises

Put a damp, cold cloth on the area. If there is a lot of swelling, ask an adult to help you.

Choking

If the person can speak, cough, and breathe, do nothing. Otherwise, stand behind the person and grasp your hands around her, just under her rib cage. Press your hands into her stomach with four quick upward moves. Do this until the person spits out the food or object.

If you are choking, move your hand across your throat to let others know. If no one is around, try pressing your hands into your stomach with four quick upward moves.

Poisoning

This is always serious and a big emergency. If you or someone you know has taken poison, or even might have taken poison, call the poison control center and your emergency first-aid number immediately.

Be very careful about what you put in your mouth. Check to make sure that the food and liquids that you buy are sealed and safety-wrapped. Food that needs to be in the refrigerator can spoil easily. Food can look and smell good and still be spoiled and make you sick. Make sure you keep this food cold.

Don't ever take any kinds of medications, drugs, or pills unless they have been prescribed to you

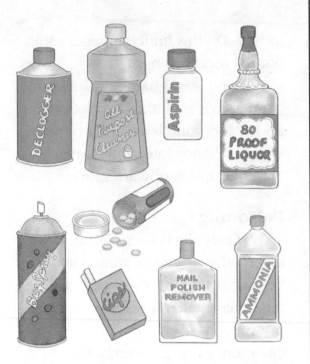

by a doctor and an adult is present. Don't drink alcohol or try cigarettes because you think it is "grown-up." Alcohol and cigarettes can be very harmful to your body.

Are You Prepared?

Practice these first-aid techniques on each other. Practice with your family and friends, too. Remember the Girl Scout motto is "Be Prepared." You need to be prepared to stay safe.

Feeling Good About Yourself

Look at the pictures. They will help you sing this song.

This song is special. It is about you. Write the words or draw the pictures in the empty spaces that will complete the song.

_____ 's SONG

My name is

_____ .

I am _____ years old.

I have my own story

And here it's told.

_____ is where I live,

My nose is right here on my face,

My favorite food is

_____ .

I am _____ inches high.

And _____ is the color of my eyes.

And _____ is my favorite game.

I've put a picture of myself,

Inside this picture frame.

And this is how loud I can shout!

Because I'm a Brownie Girl Scout!

I can _____ very well,

But I always try to do my best,

Take turns singing your special song.
Can you think of other movements
to the song?

You Are Special

You have learned many different things in this chapter. You have learned about staying safe and practicing first aid. You have learned about taking care of your body and taking care of your home. You can also take care of the person inside.

You are a very special person. No one in the entire world shares your feelings, your thoughts, your likes, and dislikes. No one looks just like you or can do all the things you can do. Even if you have a twin sister or brother, you would never be exactly the same.

Feelings

You do not feel the same way all the time. Sometimes you feel happy. Sometimes you feel sad. You can feel angry, scared, bored, excited, surprised. Why do you feel different ways at different times?

Often you can change your feelings. What are some things you can do when you feel scared?

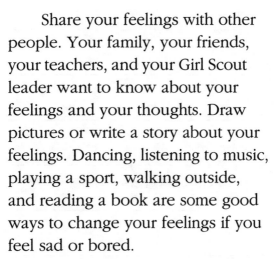

Share your feelings with other people. Your family, your friends, your teachers, and your Girl Scout leader want to know about your feelings and your thoughts. Draw pictures or write a story about your feelings. Dancing, listening to music, playing a sport, walking outside, and reading a book are some good ways to change your feelings if you feel sad or bored.

You can show how you feel in many different ways. Show how you would feel if:

- You heard someone tease you about your clothes.
- You hit the winning home run in your softball game.
- Your younger brother used your best blouse to polish his bike.
- You forgot to bring your homework to school.
- You wrote a story on the computer at school and someone accidentally erased it.

Talents and Interests

Interests are things you like, and talents are things you are good at doing. Sometimes, your interests and talents are the same. Singing is a good example. A professional singer is good at singing and likes it. Another person may like singing very much but may not be so very good at it. (She may have a lot of fun singing in the shower, though!)

Interests and talents can change as you grow older. You can work on talents that you know need improvement. You can also discover new talents. It is important to try many different types of activities so

that you can find out what talents you have. Everybody has talents. Some people might have talents that are easier to see. Being good at sports is easier to see than being good at helping people to get along with each other, but both are very important talents!

What are some things that you do very well? Write them here.

Writing
Watch T.V
math
acting
danceing
reading
spelling
skating

What interests do you have?

runing
teaching
dogs
cards
cats
Brownie

What are some things you would like to know how to do better?

What can you do with your wishes and talents?

_____

_____

_____

_____

_____

Careers

Talents and interests can lead to careers. A career is what you do as work. An interest in collecting rocks can lead to a career as a geologist, a person who studies the earth. A talent in drawing can lead to a career as a book illustrator or as an architect who plans and designs buildings. An interest in helping people might lead you to become a doctor or a teacher. A talent in sports could become a career as a coach or a sports announcer.

What possible careers match your talents and interests? Find out more about those careers. Try to find someone who is working in one of those careers. What would be some good questions to ask her?

Draw a picture of a scientist here.

Did you draw a woman? What kind of person do you think of when you think of a scientist? a firefighter? a lawyer? For a long time people thought women could not do those jobs. Now, along with those careers, women can and are doing many things that once only men did: astronauts, presidents of companies, politicians, and engineers. In fact, many of these women were Girl Scouts when they were young. What exciting career will you have?

Find out about someone who was the first woman to do what she does for a living. How did she feel? Was she treated the same way as the men who were working with her?

Family, Friends, and Neighbors

Marta looked at the big clock again. 2:32! The hands were moving so slowly. At 2:40, school was over and today was Wednesday and on Wednesdays, she could barely wait for school to finish.

Marta Makes a Choice

Marta jiggled her leg and tapped her pencil. Great, Ms. Liu was moving toward the front of the room. "Suki, what do you have to remember to do for tomorrow?"

"Write a story. About someone we admire. And why. I'm writing about Jackee Joyner-Kersee. I want to be in the Olympics, too, someday."

Dr. Tamara Jernigan became an astronaut in 1986. She flew as a mission specialist in June 1991 and is scheduled for more space flights.

"You do run fast. That's a good choice," Ms. Liu said. "Has anyone else picked someone to write about?"

Michelle raised her hand. "I'm writing about Tamara Jernigan. I'd love to be an astronaut. I could float around my space ship, land on the moon, and jump 12 feet high!"

"That's also a good choice," Ms. Liu said. "Marta, what about you? Whom have you picked?"

Marta was staring at the clock as the hand clicked to 2:40. "I don't know. I really can't think of anybody." She looked at Ms. Liu.

"Well, if you think about it, I'm sure you'll think of someone you admire enough to write about. Any questions? No? Okay, see you all tomorrow."

Marta already had her backpack in her hand. She raced to the door, swung down the hallway, and down the front steps of the school. Her grandmother was waiting at the bottom step.

"Hi, Nana," said Marta as she gave her grandmother a big hug. She could feel Nana's bones through her sweater and dress. Nana had always been short and as she got older she got thinner and shorter, but much tougher, she told Marta.

Nana wasn't really a huggy kind of person, Marta thought. But, she was always there when she was needed. "Like when my parakeet, Mandy, died," Marta thought.

"I cried and cried, but Nana helped me get a box to bury Mandy in, and helped me pick out a song to sing when I buried her and let me spend the night in her room so I could sleep under the red and blue woolen quilt she had made when she was first married."

"That quilt is over 60 years old," Nana told her. "I made it when I married your grandpa. That was before we even came to this country."

And, Nana would tell her a story about when she was a child living on a farm that had goats and geese, or when she first was married and came to the United States with her new husband.

That was why Marta loved Wednesdays. Her mother went to school on Wednesday nights, and Marta and Nana had the apartment to themselves. Nana would cook something special for the two of them, always showing Marta what to do and what kind of spices or herbs would make each dish taste extra good. As they cooked, Nana would tell stories and sing old songs, and the smell of the spices and the sounds of the stories would mix together as they traveled through Nana's past.

"It is strange. That quilt is so much older now than your grandpa." Marta had heard the story many times of how Grandpa had died when Nana was very young and Marta's mother was just a baby.

So, Nana had worked. In restaurants and people's homes, scrubbing and cleaning, and cooking and washing, until her hands were always red. Her hands were still red and the skin was rough, but no one's hands felt better than Nana's when Marta was sick or tired or sleepy.

"Weren't you ever scared, Nana?" Marta asked.

"Scared of what, Marta?" Nana asked.

"Scared of leaving your family and coming to a place where you didn't know anybody and you didn't speak English? And scared of being alone after Grandpa died? Do you still miss him?"

"I didn't have time to be scared. I was always working. Well, probably I was scared at times and lonely, too. But, I also loved your mother very much and now I have you who asks me so many questions that I never have time to feel lonely—or even think!" Nana reached over and squeezed Marta's shoulder. "So, do you have homework?" Nana asked.

"I do, and I wasn't sure how to do it, but now I know exactly what I'm going to do," Marta said.

Whom do you think Marta wrote about for her story "The Person I Admire the Most"? That's right, she wrote about her grandmother. What do you think Marta admired about her grandmother?

Family

What is a family? Your family includes the people who take care of you, help you, teach you, and love you. In a family you learn how to get along with other people. Families are different. People in your family may live with you or they may live somewhere else. You may live with two parents or one parent or other people in your family. You could live with another family and become part of a new family. You might have sisters or brothers or be an "only child" with no sisters or brothers at all. You could live with your grandmother or grandfather, aunts or uncles, nieces or nephews, stepbrothers and stepsisters, stepmothers or stepfathers, cousins, godparents

. . . even pets! There are so many different kinds of people who can make up a family!

In this space you could paste a photograph of your family or draw a picture of your family. You could write the names of the members of your family in a design that shows how everyone in your family is connected to each other.

In the Puppets, Dolls, and Plays Try-It, you can learn how to make many different kinds of puppets. Pick one type of puppet and make a set of family puppets. You can make the puppets like your own family or make puppets like a pretend family.

Use your puppets to act out these family situations:

- Something that made your family happy.
- Something that your family is planning to do.
- An activity that your family usually does together.
- Something funny that happened in your family.

• Something that made your family sad.

Can you think of some others?

In a family, you learn how to get along with other people. Families can have a lot of fun together, but families can also argue. It is not so easy when people live together to get everyone to agree all of the time! Maybe you want to watch a program on television and your brother wants to listen to music and your mother wants to read the newspaper and wants quiet! What happens? Not everybody can have her or his own way. When you live with other people, you cannot always do what you want or get your own way. You have to cooperate with each other. Cooperation means working together. How could the family cooperate in the situation above?

Think of times when families disagree. Use your puppets to act out ways to cooperate with each other.

Make a "Help My Family" promise. What promise can you make for your family? Maybe you can promise to be ready for school on time so your mother doesn't have to remind you so often. Maybe you can promise not to argue with your older brother and he can promise not to argue with you!

Things Families Do Together

Families also do things together that are fun. Families can spend a lot of time together, but during the week, many families are busy doing things apart from each other, like working or going to school. Sometimes, families plan time on the weekends to spend together. Sometimes, different members of the family are busy on the weekend, too. What are some things your family does together? What are some things you do with just one member of your family?

Think of a fun activity you can do with your family indoors. Maybe you could try a game or activity you learned in Brownie Girl Scouts.

Think of a fun activity you could do with your whole family or a member of your family outdoors.

Make a picture book, a poster, or a chart showing what an average weekday is like in the life of your family. Keep track of what is done from the time the members of your family wake up until the time you all go to bed. Share this with your family. Would you spend your time in a different way? Can you spend less time on some things and more time on others?

How does your family spend

Saturday or Sunday? Choose one of those days and keep track of how your family spends time. Share your charts with your Brownie Girl Scout group. Did you find out something new to do with your family?

What are some family jobs? Make a list of the jobs that different people in your family do in the home. Who cooks? Who cleans? Who does the shopping? Try making a kaper chart for your family. What are your own family responsibilities?

Try making a special box or jar for family jobs. Write the names of jobs or draw small pictures on slips of paper and put them inside the box or jar. Family members can choose different jobs each week.

What are some special days you celebrate with your family? Talk about holidays and celebrations with your Brownie Girl Scout group.

Why not create a group holiday celebration? Each person can share a food, decoration, song, or tradition from her favorite holiday.

Families may also have times that are not fun. Sometimes parents don't live together. Sometimes parents get divorced. Maybe a grandparent dies. If you have a pet, you will feel sad if your pet runs away. Maybe your mother loses her job. These things may happen. Sometimes, girls your age worry about these things happening when they won't really happen. If you have worries like this, you should talk to people in your family and other people you love. Remember, you have people who love you very much and will listen to you if you are worried or sad.

Family History

Families celebrate holidays in different ways because families often have different backgrounds. Maybe people came from other countries. Maybe people came from different parts of the United States. Find out more about your family.

- Where were your family members born?
- Where were your ancestors (people like your great-grandparents, and their grandparents) born?
- How did your parents celebrate holidays when they were children?
- Are there any recipes, songs, dances, or customs from long ago that your family still shares?

If you can, think of questions to ask the oldest person in your family—or an older person who shares your cultural background or who has lived in the same place as you for a long time. Find a way to keep a record of this person's answers. You could use a tape recorder, a video recorder, or you could make a scrapbook.

Share your family history with your Brownie Girl Scout group. Can you make a story or a play? Can you re-tell a special story from your family? Can you act out something that happened to a person in the past?

Find out more about families which have the same background as yours and those which have different backgrounds. You could look for books in a library, visit a museum, go to an ethnic festival, or watch a movie or play.

FRIENDS

Friends are important. Friends can act like a family. They can help you and take care of you. You go places together and you learn new things. You may have many friends, or you may have one or two friends. Sometimes you may get along and sometimes you may not. You may like people for different reasons. You can have friends who are a lot like you and you can have friends who are different.

Just as people in families may come from different places, so do friends. Maybe you have a friend who was born in a different part of the world, or who is older or younger than you, or who has different eye, skin, or hair color than you have. Having friends who are different from you makes a friendship interesting. Think of how much you can learn from each other. Imagine how boring life would be if all your friends were just like you!

- What are three things I can learn from my friends?
- What are three things I can teach my friends?

Friends with Different Abilities

You and your friends have different abilities. An ability is something you can do. Maybe you can run faster than your friend, but she can read faster than you do. Everybody you meet has some things she does well and some things she

(continued on page 77)

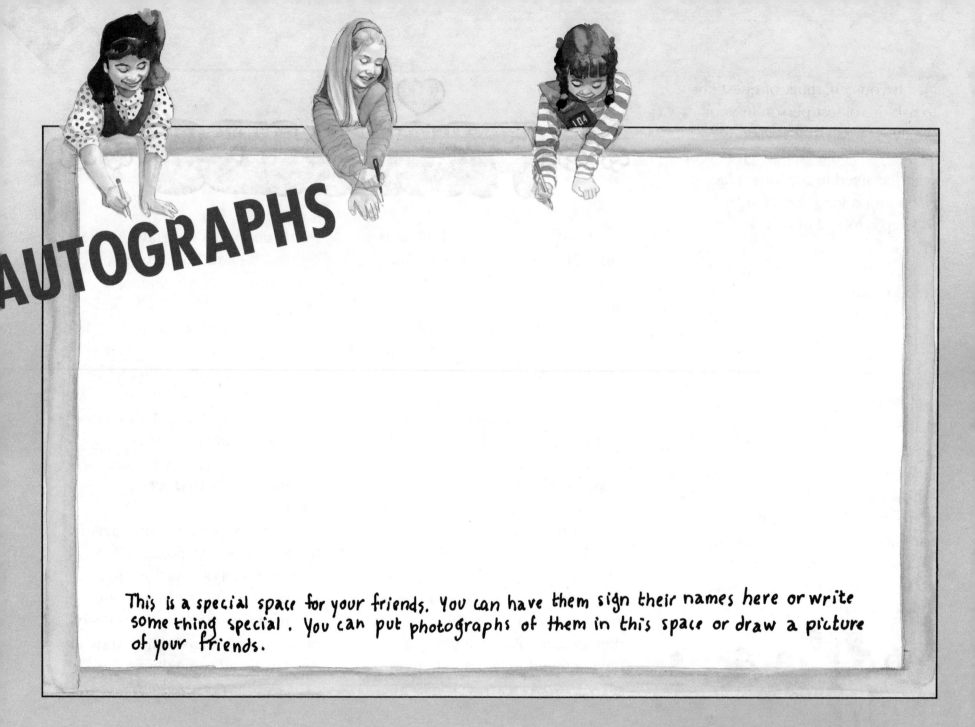

AUTOGRAPHS

This is a special space for your friends. You can have them sign their names here or write something special. You can put photographs of them in this space or draw a picture of your friends.

doesn't do well. Some of your friends may have a disability. Maybe you have a disability. A disability is something that may make it harder for a person to do some things.

A person who is blind cannot see. She may use her hearing or her touch to help her know more about the world. She may use a cane or a seeing eye dog to help move about. A person who is deaf may hear some sounds, but not very clearly, or may hear no sounds. She may look at the lips of people who are talking and figure out what people are saying. This is called lip-reading. If you are deaf, you may have a special machine for your television or telephone so you can read what people are saying.

You might have a disability that makes it hard to walk. You might need a wheelchair or crutches or a leg brace to help you walk. These disabilities are easy to see. You could also have a disability that is not easy to see, like a learning disability. A learning disability may make it hard

to learn how to read and write. You could also have a disability that makes it difficult to pay attention or to sit still.

Visit a place in your neighborhood that helps people who have disabilities or find out about a career working with people who have disabilities.

Learn more about some of the helpful tools for people with disabilities. Wheelchairs, hearing aids, walkers, leg braces, canes, artificial limbs, eyeglasses, reading machines, computers, talking books, and video machines are just some.

Here are some activities that will help you understand disabilities you might not have.

Blind walk. This activity will help you feel what it is like to be unable to see. Have a partner blindfold you and walk around with you slowly to make sure you don't get hurt. Stop to feel things. Use your senses of touch, hearing, and smell to learn about your environment. What happens to your other senses when you cannot see?

Learn a new language. Try wearing earphones or headphones for part of your Brownie Girl Scout meeting. How does it feel? How did you know what was being said? People who cannot hear often learn how to use sign language. There are different systems of sign language.

Use the sign alphabet chart to figure out the message on the facing page.

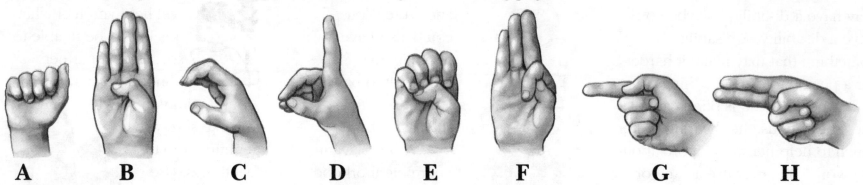

A   B   C   D   E   F   G   H

I   J   K   L   M   N   O   P   Q

R   S   T   U   V   W   X   Y   Z

Each hand position stands for a letter.

Practice making words with this new alphabet. If you meet someone who cannot hear, you'll be able to "talk" with her or him if she or he knows this alphabet.

Mirror image. Some people have trouble learning how to read. Letters may look mixed up to them. It's hard for them to make sense out of words on the page. This condition is called dyslexia (dis-lek-see-uh).

To see what this disability is like, try to read the message below.

THIS IS HARD TO READ

To figure out what this message says, hold the page up to a mirror. Imagine how it must feel to have to learn to read when everything looks so mixed up! However, most people who have reading disabilities can and do learn to read.

Dress yourself. Put on a man's shirt—unbuttoned. Put a pair of thick socks or very thick mittens on your hands and try to button the shirt. What happens? This will show you how someone who cannot move her body easily could have a hard time getting dressed. What kind of clothing would be easier to wear?

Being a Friend

Learning to be a friend is an important part of Girl Scouting. To have a friend, you must be a friend. How can you be a friend to someone? What do the Girl Scout Promise and Law tell you about friendship?

I am a friend when I _____

_____

_____

I am not a friend when I _____

_____

_____

_____

_____

When you are talking with your family, friends, or people you have just met, there are ways to make sure they understand what you are saying.

1. Be a good listener. Listen to every word the person says. Decide if the person is telling you something, asking you something, or just sharing what's on her mind. If you are not sure what the person is saying, try saying it back to her in a different way. You can say, "I think you said. . . ."

2. Think about what you say and how you say it. Does your voice sound angry? Do you give the other person a chance to speak? Do you treat your listener the way you would like to be treated? As a Girl Scout, part of the Law you are trying to live by is "to show respect for myself and others through my words and actions."

Here are some activities to help practice talking with people:

- Keep a diary for a day. Write how people acted when you listened carefully to what they said.
- Make a list of ways to show respect for others. For example: I show respect by not making fun of what someone said. I show respect when I listen carefully.

- When you and your friend do not agree about how to do something, what do you do? Think of a time that you and a friend didn't agree. What did you do? How did you make up?
- How would you solve the following problems?

1. You and two friends are in the playground and there is one jump-rope left.

2. Your friend doesn't want you to invite the new girl in your Brownie Girl Scout troop to your birthday party.

3. The older girls in your troop tease you because you cannot write well.

Sometimes our friends do things they should not do. They may think you should do it too. This is a time when being a friend is very hard. You must remember what is right and what is wrong, and then do what you know is right. Even if it means that you get teased or called names, you should never do something you know is wrong because other people want you to do it.

With friends or in your troop, think of some situations when people might ask you to do something you know is wrong. What can you say to them? Practice what you would say in each situation.

Things Friends Do Together

There are many things you can do with your friends. Playing games and sports are good ways to keep fit. Games and sports often have rules to follow. You should play fair and always try to do your best. Having fun is the most important thing, not who wins or loses.

Here are some games you can play with your friends. Can you think of some others? You can look in the *Games for Girl Scouts* book for more ideas.

Initials

Two or more players are needed. One player is chosen to be the "questioner" for the first round.

The questioner asks each player a question. The player must answer the question with an answer formed from the initials of her own name. If the questioner asks, "What is your favorite food, Rosa Carlo?" Rosa may answer, "Red cherries," or "Raisin cake." If the questioner asks, "How do you like to spend Saturday morning, Shelly Steinberg?" Shelly may answer, "Simply sleeping," or "Singing songs." The answers don't have to make sense. Actually it is more fun if they don't. If you repeat an answer or can't think of an answer, you are out. The last player becomes the questioner for the next round.

Invent your own games and play them with others. Try making a game in which everyone wins, like cooperative musical chairs. You still take a chair away in each turn, but everyone tries to sit on the chairs that are left, until you only have one chair and everyone tries to sit on it!

Here are some games that you can play with just one other person.

Make a Box

Draw 40 dots on a piece of paper. Each player takes a turn drawing a line between two dots that are next to each other. The first player to make a box puts her name or initials in the box. You keep playing until all the dots are connected or until one person gets ten boxes. The person who makes the most boxes is the winner.

New Games from Old

Take out a chess or checkers set and invent a new game with your own rules. For example, you can make a rule that the checkers must be moved diagonally or two spaces at a time. Or, you can give the different pieces of a chess set different kinds of movements or give them all the same movements.

Your Friends and School

Many Brownie Girl Scouts spend a lot of their time in school. School gives you a chance to meet many friends and do fun things together. You can work on a class project, play an instrument in the school band, sing in the chorus, play softball, or put on a play together.

MY SCHOOL STORY

Fill in the blanks below. Remember to add on pages as you move from year to year in Brownie Girl Scouting.

Name of my school

_____

Name of my teacher

_____

Names of friends in my class

_____

Number of grades or age levels

_____

Number of students in school

_____

Number of students in class

_____

My favorite school subject

_____

Draw a picture of or paste a photograph of your school, or describe it in the space above.

Your Neighbors and Neighborhood

Who are the people you see every day? The people who live near you in your community are your neighbors. A neighborhood is all of the people, all of the streets, all of the buildings, parks, and other places near your home.

Make a Neighborhood Map

Try making a map of a part of your neighborhood that you like. You can pick the streets near your home or near your school or near your Brownie Girl Scout meeting place. You can choose a park or an open space. How will you show the different buildings, streets, trees, and other special things in your neighborhood?

Maps have legends. The legend is the list of what different drawings

Here is the space for your map.

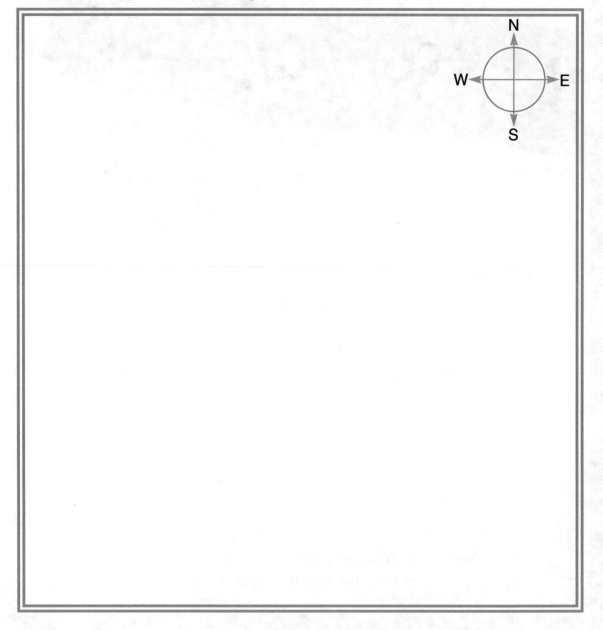

mean on your map. Here are some examples.

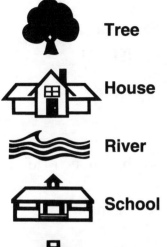

Tree

House

River

School

Office building

What kind of legend can you make for your map? Share your map with other people who know your neighborhood.

Explore Your Neighborhood

Explore your neighborhood. Ask an adult or someone older than you to walk with you. Look for things that are:

Old _____

_____

New _____

_____

Made by people _____

_____

Natural _____

_____

Big _____

_____

Small _____

_____

People in Your Neighborhood

Who are the neighbors you could meet visiting places in your neighborhood? What kinds of jobs would these neighbors have? Do some of your neighbors have jobs where they can help people? How did they get these jobs? What school and training did they need? What else can you find out? Why not interview a neighborhood worker or ask her or him to visit your troop?

Be a Telephone Book Detective

Your telephone book can also give you a lot of information about your neighborhood. Find out if some people have the same last name as you. How many different names can you find?

What are the most common names? What can names tell you about the people who live in your neighborhood? If you can get to a library, find out if it has copies of old phone books. Compare the old phone books with the new ones. What information can you discover about your neighborhood?

Hidden Neighborhood Workers

The scrambled words on the right answer the questions about neighborhood workers on the left. First unscramble the words, then answer the questions.

1. Who makes sure that people obey traffic laws?

   a. gdo ccahetr

2. Who puts out fires?

   b. ehoteepln reptaoro

3. Who gives you health checkups and vaccinations?

   c. coliep

4. Who gives you the correct telephone number?

   d. bamanlecu vidrer

5. Who collects garbage and trash and cleans the street?

   e. blairarin

6. Who keeps stray animals from running loose?

   f. erfi fghitre

7. Who checks to see that your teeth and gums are healthy?

   g. tnidtse

8. Who will drive you to the hospital in an emergency?

   h. rapk greran

9. Who helps you find your favorite book?

   i. codrot

10. Who helps you discover more about parks and green spaces?

    j. nstiaonait krorwe

Answer key: dogcatcher, telephone operator, police, ambulance driver, fire fighter, dentist, doctor, sanitation worker, librarian, park ranger.

People Near and Far

World Trefoil Pin

When you became a Brownie Girl Scout, you became part of a very big family! Girl Scouts in the United States are members of the World Association of Girl Guides and Girl Scouts. In countries all around the world, you have sisters who are members of the world movement of Girl Guiding and Girl Scouting. The World Trefoil pin may be worn by all Girl Scouts and Girl Guides.

In this chapter are stories about Ananse Guides, Bluebird Girl Scouts, Alita Girl Scouts, and Grønsmutte Girl Scouts. The first story is about the Ananse Guides, which is what Brownie Girl Scouts in Ghana, West Africa, are called. Ananse is a spider. Why would you name Girl Scouts after a spider? Because Ananse is a very, very smart spider and many stories are told in West Africa about Ananse. Remember in "Welcome to Girl Scouts," you read a story about brownies? In Ghana, Ananse Guides read a story about Ananse the spider.

Ananse's Gift

In the middle of the forest there was a small house under an oil palm tree. A grandmother and two grandchildren, a boy and a girl, lived in this house. They were twins and named Abena One and Abena Two, which is how twins were named.

When Abena One and Abena Two were in school, the grandmother would walk to her farm and dig and weed and pick some vegetables for dinner.

One day, the children came home and saw an empty cooking pot. "Where's our dinner?" they asked.

Grandmother looked at the children. "I have worked hard, but now my back is bent and my arms are weak. I can't dig and I can't weed. Unless I get new arms and a new back, I can't bring home food anymore."

That night Abena One and Abena Two went to their beds, but they couldn't sleep. They waited until their grandmother was sleeping, and very quietly went outside.

"We must get our grandmother new arms and a new back. Let's go and ask the Wise One what we should do."

They walked into the forest where they saw a tiny house. From the house came two high, squeaky voices, singing this song, "Here they come, come one, come two. What's the good they want to do?"

Abena One and Abena Two looked in the doorway. They saw two small people with so many hands and so many feet that the children knew they had found Ananse and his wife.

Without getting up, Ananse waved the children into the room with two of his hands. At the same time, he used another two hands to pull up two chairs and put two mugs on the table with two more hands!

Ananse asked them what they wanted. Abena One and Two explained that their grandmother needed new arms and a new back.

Ananse folded two arms on the table. He used two more arms to scratch his head as he thought and then patted Abena One on the back with one arm and Abena Two on the back with another. He looked at his wife.

She spoke, "We are very clever, but even Ananse cannot give new arms and new backs. But, don't worry. I know a secret. The Good God has already answered your wish."

She took the children outside. "Close your eyes."

Ananse took Abena One's hands and put them on Abena Two's back. Abena One said, "That's a fine strong back for my grandmother."

Then Ananse's wife took Abena Two and put his hands on the arms of Abena One. Abena Two said, "Those are fine strong arms for my grandmother."

BOOOM! A big clap of thunder filled the sky and when the children opened their eyes, they were all alone. Ananse, his wife, and the little house had disappeared!

The next morning the children woke up early and walked to the farm. They weeded and raked. They picked just enough vegetables for dinner. When they got home, they swept the yard, started the cooking fire, and started a delicious soup. The smell of the soup drifted into the house and the grandmother woke up.

"What is that wonderful smell?" she said. Then she saw the soup bubbling over the fire and the yard so clean and neat. She looked at the children. "We did it, Grandmother. We visited Ananse the Spider. We learned that we could be your arms and your back. Now you never have to worry."

Before they went to school each day, Abena One and Abena Two worked on the farm. Soon, they had the best farm in the village. They kept the yard and the house very clean—except for one small corner by the back door. In that corner was a shiny web and two small busy spiders who looked very much like Ananse and his wife.

Do you know any folk tales? A folk tale is a kind of story that shows you how to behave or how something happened. Maybe someone in your family knows some folk tales. Why not have a folk tale story hour in your Brownie Girl Scout troop or group meeting? Can you make up your own folk tale? It might be fun to make some new folk tales and act them out.

Ananse Guides in Ghana

If you were an Ananse Girl Guide, you would probably speak English and another local language. Most people in Ghana speak two or more languages. You could live in a city, a suburb, or the country. Wherever you lived, it would be hot most of the year. Half the year would have rainy weather and half the year would have dry weather.

In the country, you might live on a cocoa farm. Do you know what you can make out of cocoa? Chocolate! You might shop in a supermarket or an open market. On tables, you could see bananas, coconuts, peanuts, rice, mangoes and papaya, other foods, and things for the house, like soap, brushes, and dishes. Some fruits and vegetables would be hard to find in the United States, like soursop. It sounds funny, but it tastes cool and sweet and makes great ice cream! You could walk through the market, listening to people greeting

each other and buying their food, smelling all kinds of fruits and vegetables, and seeing so many bright colors. Maybe you would help your mother when you came home from school with her market table. In Ghana, women make much money for their families because they sell the food they grow or the things they make in the market.

At one time, Ghana had a marvelous empire, called the Songhai, with large palaces in which princesses and princes lived. People came from all over the world to sell and buy things. Many people would trade—give one thing to get a different thing. For example, a trader might want salt. He has iron. He would give the salt seller the iron and get the salt in trade. Today, Ghana is still famous for its markets.

Can you and your Brownie Girl Scout troop make a market? What could you bring in to trade? You could bring crafts you have made, food you have prepared, or other things that you think someone else

would like. What rules would you set up for trading? How would you set up the tables?

If you make some peanut or coconut cookies or some banana bread, or a fruit salad with bananas, oranges, and coconut, you could eat what Ananse Girl Guides like to eat. Hot chocolate would be a good thing to drink.

Adinkra Cloth

Ghana is famous for its beautiful cloth, especially a kind called Adinkra cloth. Stamps are made from a kind of gourd, a calabash. Each stamp has a different meaning. Different stamps make beautiful designs and tell a story.

Adinkra cloth is usually divided into squares. You can make your stamps from hard foam or from a square eraser. Use a plastic knife to make your patterns. Traditionally, Adinkra cloth has black stamps, so you could use black poster paint. Press your stamps into the paint and then onto white construction paper or pieces of a white cotton sheet. If you want to wear the cloth, use acrylic or water-fast paint. Share stamps with your friends for different designs.

Bluebird Girl Guides in Thailand

Bluebirds are Brownie Girl Scouts in Thailand. Thailand is in Southeast Asia. Bluebirds go to Flock

meetings with a Flock leader. If a girl wants to join a Flock, she is called a Fledgling, a baby bird. She has ten different things to do and if she does them, she gets a Blue Feather. Then she does ten more things—a little harder than the first— and gets her Silver Feather. And then, she can do eight more for a Golden Feather!

After three years in a Flock, just like your three years in Brownie Girl Scouts, a Bluebird flies away to Girl Guides, just as you would fly up to Junior Girl Scouts.

Thailand has mountains with forests and jungles, beautiful beaches, big and little cities, and many farms that grow rice. Elephants are common animals in Thailand and are used to help do work, like pulling logs or moving heavy things.

People in Thailand speak Thai and many people also speak French or English. The Thai language has a different alphabet than English and a different sound. The same word can have different meanings if you say it in a high voice or a low voice, so the language sounds very musical and beautiful. Here is the Bluebird motto, "Be Prepared," in the Thai language written with an English alphabet:

Chuey luer poo uen smer

Kite Festival

A very special holiday that Bluebirds look forward to is the Kite Festival. The Thai people make big and small kites in many bright colors and many unusual shapes. Some kites look like butterflies and some kites look like birds. Some even look like dragons! Imagine a sunny blue sky full of these kites!

Why not make your own kites? Look on pages 222–223 in the Movers Try-It. Decorate your kite with elephants or dragons or birds with bright feathers and you can have a kite that a Bluebird might fly.

Crayon Resist

Batik

Silk is colored with beautiful patterns in Thailand. One way to make patterns on cloth is called batik. You put wax on cloth and dip it in different colors. When you take the wax off, the design you made appears!

You can use crayons to do something similar on paper. Crayons and paint together are called "resist." You will need white paper, white crayons, and different kinds of water-colors. Make a design on the white paper with your white crayon. Press hard so that the crayon sticks to the paper. Then, paint the paper with bright watercolors. Your "resist" design will show through the paint. Try using other light colors of crayons to make your designs.

Alita Girl Guides in Peru

In Peru, Brownie Girl Scouts are called Alitas, which means "Little Wing." Many people speak Spanish and some people speak two languages, Spanish and a local language. Alitas say their Promise in Spanish:

Prometo hacer todo lo posible por cumplir mis deberes para con Dios y mi Patria.

Ayudar a otras personas, especialmente a los de casa.

Do you speak Spanish? Can you read the Alitas Promise in the Spanish spoken in Peru? Try singing this folk song from Peru that an Alita might sing.

Peru is a large country in South America. If you were an Alita, you could live in high mountains, the Andes, covered with snow, or near dry deserts, the rain forest, or near many beaches. Maybe you would live on a farm, or in the capital city, Lima. In the country, you would be able to see llamas and alpacas, members of the camel family. Llamas help carry heavy loads and alpacas have long, soft hair used to make beautiful clothing and blankets.

Los Maizales

Peru
Folk Song

Los mai - za - les bro - tan con pri - mor
ful - gu - ran sus ho - jas de co - lor;
La tie - rra fer - til, el sol be - só,
su be - llo gra - no ger - mi - nó.
Tie - rra Pe - rua - na de_ho - nor te_em - bria - gas.

2. Después de la faena intelectual
   vamos presurosos a jugar,
   Cual nuestros padres al son de pan,
   vamos el campo a cultivar.
   Tierra Peruana, de honor te
   embriagas.

This song describes the beauty of the cornfields and suggests that all Peruvians should help with the task of "growing their bread."

Setting up Loom

Diagonal Stripe

Chevron Stripe

Finger Weaving

Finger weaving is one way to use alpaca yarn to make colorful belts. Follow these directions to finger weave your own belt.

You will need about 20 lengths of heavy yarn in one color and 20 lengths of heavy yarn in another color. (More yarn makes a wider belt. Less yarn makes a narrower belt.) You will also need a pencil. Measure your waist and cut the yarn long enough to go around your waist and make a fringe and a knot.

Tie the yarns on the pencil with enough left over for the fringe. Tie the yarns on top together and tie or tape to the back of a chair, a door-knob, a shelf, or something else to keep your weaving in one place.

Start with the piece of yarn (strand) on the left and weave it over and under until it comes out on the right side. Always start on the left. Always follow the over and under pattern. Keep the yarn even and straight, but don't pull it too tightly.

The Inca

If you were an Alita, you might be descended from the Inca. A long, long time ago, around 1500 A.D., a people called the Inca ruled all the lands around Peru. Many different kinds of people who spoke different languages were ruled by the Inca. The Inca built more than 10,000 miles of roads and many big cities made of stone. These cities were so well-made that some of the buildings are still there. Steps were cut into the high mountains so runners could travel faster. Runners would be ready to run from city to city to spread news and carry messages. A team of runners could travel over 1,000 miles in one week!

Do you know how far 1,000 miles is? It is approximately the distance between Washington, D.C., and Savannah, Georgia! What city is 1,000 miles away from the place you live? What other cities are 1,000 miles apart?

The weaving that people in Peru do today was also very important to the Inca. Bridges that stretched high in the sky were made of woven rope! Accountants kept track of how much gold or how many potatoes were in a warehouse or how many people lived in a city on complex knotted strings called quipus. Clothing was woven to each person's exact shape. Reed plants were woven to make boats and another kind of reed plant was woven to make roofs for houses. Large woven fishnets were used in the ocean and in lakes. Incan soldiers knew how to weave and could make their own woven armor. Armor is special heavy clothing worn by soldiers that makes it less likely they will be hurt.

Make a Simple Loom

Here are the directions for making a simple loom. Try weaving a purse that an Alita might carry with her.

You need cardboard, yarn, and a heavy needle for weaving or a long narrow piece of cardboard with a hole cut in one end (shuttle).

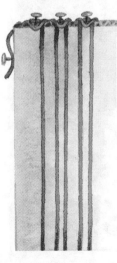

Cut two pieces of cardboard the exact size you want your weaving to be when you are done. Glue the two pieces together. Put a piece of tape over the top edge. Place an even number of pins about one-quarter-inch apart. (You can put your pins closer together if your yarn is thin. Just remember to put your pins in evenly. Use a ruler to help measure.)

You will use two types of threads. Warp threads go up and down (vertically). Weft threads go from side to side (horizontally). Weft threads weave over and under, over and under. Warp threads stay fixed. The diagram shows you how to attach your warp threads.

Put your weft yarn onto your needle or cardboard shuttle. Start weaving over and under at the lower right-hand corner. When you are all the way across, turn the loom over

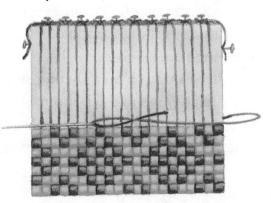

and keep going over and under until you reach the place you started. Keep going around the loom until you are done.

A comb will help you keep your threads straight and your weaving neat.

If you weave on only one side and attach pins on the bottom of your loom, you can weave a place-mat, a bookmark, or a wall hanging.

How can you make different designs in your weaving?

Grønsmutte Girl Scouts in Denmark

In Denmark, Brownie Girl Scouts are Grønsmutte, which is a wren—a small bird. They are also known as Brownie Girl Guides. Grønsmutte have the motto:

Vi vil sta sammen.

Vi vil gore vort bedste.

The poem is in Danish, the language spoken by many Grønsmutte. It means, "We will stick together. We will do our best." Grønsmutte speak Danish but also learn English in school. Here are some words in Danish:

Good day	God Dag	(Go-day)
Goodbye	Farvel	(Far-vel)
Thank you	Tak	(Tak)

Do you know how to say these words in another language? If you do, why not teach them to your Brownie Girl Scout troop/group?

Hans Christian Andersen

Denmark is a country in the north of Europe. It is flat with lakes and woods and farms and ocean beaches. Denmark is famous for beautiful china and furniture, good food, and a very famous writer who loved children—Hans Christian Andersen. You probably know some of his stories—*The Little Mermaid*, *Thumbelina*, *The Ugly Duckling*, *The Wild Swans*, and *The Princess and the Pea*. The Danish people loved his stories so much that they put a statue of the Little Mermaid in the harbor of their capital city, Copenhagen.

The tales that Hans Christian Andersen wrote were usually about a person who has a problem and has to find some way, usually through wonderful adventures, to solve her problem. She might get help from others. She might learn something special. His stories almost always had a happy ending.

Here's room to write your own story:

Once upon a time...

Why not try making up some actions to go along with your story? You could mime (actions without words) while someone else reads.

Things Danish Brownie Girl Scouts Like to Do

Danish Brownie Girl Scouts like to play games, just like you. If you were a Danish Brownie Girl Scout, you might play these games.

Good Morning, Good Afternoon, Good Evening

With your friends, make a circle. You run around the outside of the circle and tap one girl on the back as you pass. She runs the opposite way around the circle. When you meet, you each give the Brownie Girl Scout salute and say "Good Morning." Keep running until you meet again, give the salute and say "Good Afternoon." Run around one more time, stop, shake hands, say "Good Evening," and then run to the empty place on the circle.

Fruit Salad

Sit on chairs in a circle. The apple-woman stands in the middle. She does not have a chair. Everyone else has the name of a fruit (orange, banana, pineapple, etc.) If the apple-woman yells "Oranges," all the oranges change places and the apple-woman tries to find a chair. If the apple-woman calls "Fruit Salad!" everyone gets up and finds a new place to sit.

Make a Danish Open-Faced Sandwich

Playing a game called "Fruit Salad" could make a Danish Brownie Girl Scout think of food. One of her favorites would be open-faced sandwiches. They are easy to make and so good to eat. Why not try some?

You will need:

- Thin slices of buttered bread (or margarine)
- Toppings:
  Thin slices of Danish cheese
  Thin slices of ham or chicken
  Sardines or herring
  Slices of hard-boiled egg
- Garnish (makes the sandwich look nice):
  Small slices/pieces of cucumber, tomato, lemon, radish, parsley, watercress, green pepper, dill

Your sandwich will have three parts: a slice of buttered bread, a topping, and a garnish. Mix and match to make many different kinds of sandwiches. Just remember not to put a piece of bread on top!

Games from Around the World

Not only do children in Denmark love to play games, but children all around the world love to play games, too. Many of the games that you play are played in other countries.

Rabbit Without a House (Brazil)

This Brazilian game is best when you have at least 11 people.

1. Pick someone to be "it" (the rabbit without a house) and someone to be the caller.

2. Divide the others into groups of three.

3. Each group makes a rabbit in a house by two girls holding hands (the house) and one girl (a rabbit) standing inside.

4. The caller yells out "Find a house" and all the rabbits, including the one without a house, have to run to find another house.

5. The rabbit left without a house becomes it.

Jan-ken-pon (Japan)

You'll need two players.

1. Two players face each other with their hands behind them.

2. Together, they say "jan-ken-pon." On "pon," both bring a hand forward to stand for a stone (a fist), paper (flat hand), or scissors (V-shape with the index finger and middle finger).

3. Stone beats scissors because it can break them. Scissors beat paper because they can cut it. Paper beats stone because it can wrap up the stone.

4. A player gets a point each time her hand beats the other's. The first player who gets seven points wins.

Mr. Bear (Sweden)

You'll need at least three people, a place for "home," and the bear's den.

1. One person is Mr. Bear. He is trying to sleep in his den.

2. The other players sneak up to Mr. Bear and whisper, "Mr. Bear, are you awake?"

3. Mr. Bear pretends not to hear them. Then the players yell, "MR. BEAR, ARE YOU AWAKE?" This makes Mr. Bear furious! He chases them all and tries to catch them before they reach home, which is the safe place.

4. Everyone tagged by the bear before reaching home becomes Mr. Bear's cubs. They go back to the den with Mr. Bear.

5. When the remaining players come back to wake up Mr. Bear again, the cubs help Mr. Bear catch them.

6. When everyone has been caught, Mr. Bear picks someone else to take his place.

Hawk and Hens (Zimbabwe)

You'll need at least four people and two safety zones.

1. One person is the hawk.

2. All the other players are hens.

3. The hawk stands between the safety zones and tries to catch the hens as they run back and forth from one safety zone to the other.

4. When a hen is caught, she sits on the side and watches the game.

5. The last hen to be caught by the hawk becomes the next hawk.

Art from Around the World

Just as you enjoy creating things, children all over the world enjoy drawing and painting, singing and dancing. You have already learned a little about art in Ghana, Thailand, Peru, and Denmark. The Brownie Girl Scout Try-Its on pages 166–277 have more kinds of artwork for you to try. Here are some more.

Clay Birds from Mexico

You will need some self-hardening clay, or clay that can be hardened in a low-temperature oven overnight.

People in Mexico have made clay figures for many centuries. One of the most popular figures is a clay bird. Other animal shapes are also made.

Try making your own animal shapes. Once the clay has hardened, try painting designs on the clay with acrylic paints or

poster paints. Once the paint is dry, you can protect your clay with a special coating made for clay. An adult will have to help you with this step.

Greek Mosaics

In ancient Greece, tiny bits of colored glass and stone were cut and put into cement. Mosaics were often used to decorate the floors and walls of a home. Later, the art of making mosaics spread all around the world.

You will need different colors of construction paper and black or dark blue construction paper for the background.

With a ruler and a pencil, put a mark every half-inch along the short side of the colored construction paper. Then, do the same on the long side. Draw the lines. You will have one-half-inch squares. Cut them out. Keep all the squares of the same color in a dish or bowl.

Now, choose your paper tiles to make your mosaic and paste them on the dark paper in a design.

Tie-Dyeing

Tie-dyeing is a way of making cloth that has many colors. Tie-dyeing is done in many countries in South America, India, and China. It is also very common in the countries in West Africa, like Liberia, Senegal, Sierra Leone, and the Ivory Coast.

To tie-dye, you will need some plain white cotton cloth, different colors of fabric dye, some strong rubber bands, and basins of water or a sink for dyeing.

Tie the rubber bands around the cloth in different ways. You can dip the cloth in one color, undo the rubber bands, retie them in new places, and then dip the cloth again. Make sure the cloth is dry before you untie it. You may want to try different designs on small pieces of cloth first.

Do not take the cloth out of the dye until it is a little darker than the color you want it to be when it is dry. Rinse out the extra dye under running water or in a big basin. Change the water between rinses. Again, make sure the cloth is dry before you untie it.

To make a wall hanging, iron the cloth and then glue it to a long stick.

1.

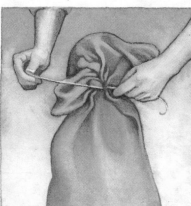

Tie rubber bands or string around cloth in different ways.

2.

Dip the cloth into a pail of dye.

3.

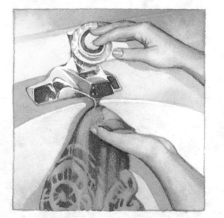

Rinse the cloth twice in cold water and hang it up to dry.

4.

Make sure the cloth is dry before you untie it.

Storytelling

Almost every country has stories. Stories are often a way to pass along information or to entertain a group of people. Families have been sharing stories long before there was television or electricity. In West Africa, storytellers were called griots and passed down family histories from one generation to the next. Many American Indian groups have stories and folk tales that teach lessons and entertain. A famous character in some of the American Indian stories from the West is Coyote.

Coyote and the Moon

It was nighttime and Coyote was hungry. "I haven't eaten all day. What I would really like is a nice round corncake. I don't want to cook one. Maybe I can very quietly find a family cooking their dinner and quickly grab a cake!"

As you can see, Coyote was very lazy and not very nice at all.

Looking ahead, he saw a family sitting near their fire. They were just on the other side of the lake. He thought, "Good, I can almost taste that cake now."

He went along the side of the lake very slowly. He looked down, and there, in the lake, he saw a big, round shiny corn cake. "What luck!" he thought. "Those people left their corncake in the lake. I'll just help myself now."

So, he reached down for the corncake, but as he touched the water, the cake broke into many pieces and then disappeared. He tried again and again and the same thing happened. He sat back, very angry and very hungry, and looked up.

"Oh, no," he said. "How did that corncake get in the sky? Maybe the family wanted to keep it safe from me. Now I am really hungry." And he put his head back and cried.

That is why when you sometimes hear the Coyote crying at the moon, you know it's because he still wants his corncake!

THE WOMAN WITH EIGHT CHILDREN

A STORY FROM THE ARAPAHO NATION

Many, many years ago, in a large forest, a woman lived with her eight children. The children loved to sing and dance all day long, never stopping for a minute except to eat.

Well, the woman got angrier and angrier that all the children would do is dance and sing and never help her with cooking or cleaning or getting wood for the fire. So one day, when they were dancing in a circle, laughing and singing, she raised her broom and shook it at them.

"I'll hit you with my broom if you don't stop dancing," she shouted.

Whoosh! Up into the beautiful night sky rose the children. The woman tried to catch them, but she could only touch the foot of one boy with her broom.

The boy fell back to earth, but when he hit the ground he was turned into a tree! His arms and legs became tree branches and his fingers became the twigs.

The other children rose higher and higher, still laughing and dancing until they formed a shape like this in the night sky.

You may see them on a starry night, twinkling as they dance and sing.

More About Storytelling

Many stories were used to explain the things that happen in nature, like thunder and lightning, big winds, or earthquakes. Can you make up a story about nature?

Many communities have someone who is good at telling stories. Find out if she or he can come to a troop meeting.

Try telling some stories yourself. Telling stories is a little different than writing stories. Try to choose words and actions that are easy to see or easy to act out. Why not have a storytelling hour at home or at a meeting?

More About People

Now you know a lot more about different kinds of people. People are the same in many ways. Everyone needs food and water and a place to live. Most people want to love somebody else and want other people to love them. They also want to feel good about themselves and be the best people that they can be.

People are also very different. Your family background, your religion, your race, your culture, the place you live, your friends, and many, many other things make you unique. Unique means different from everybody else. Differences among people are what make the world an interesting place. When different people with different ideas get together, they discover better ideas and better ways to do things. There is no one "right" way to live, look, talk, dress, eat, or act.

Just as the world contains many different types of people, so does the United States. In the chapter "Family, Friends, and Neighbors," you learned a little more about the people in your community. What did you find out? Even if you did not find so many different types of people in your neighborhood or community, you will find many different types of people in the United States. As you grow older, you may go to school in a new place or get a job in another place or marry someone who lives in another part of the country. You will meet many people different from you.

The United States of America

Your country, the United States of America, is special. It is a country of American Indians, Inuits and Aleuts from Alaska, Hawaiians from Hawaii, and other people who come from all parts of the world and bring their individual ways with them. The United States is like a mosaic made up of many different little pieces that come together to make a beautiful picture.

United States of America Montage

To make a montage of the United States of America, you will need to find pictures and drawings that show the different parts of the country. Look for pictures of mountains, forests, lakes, rivers, and deserts. Also look for pictures and drawings that show the many people who live in the United States. Make sure the drawings and pictures you find show how people really look and live. Sometimes, the pictures in books can be untrue.

Add your own drawings and words to show how we all live in the United States of America. You will also need poster paper, scissors, and glue.

1. Decide where to put the pictures on the poster.

2. Glue everything in place.

3. Show your montage to your friends.

People Different from You

When someone doesn't know a lot about people who are different from him, he may get afraid or confused and may even dislike these other people. Isn't it silly not to like someone you don't even know? This bad feeling is called prejudice. People are not born with prejudice. But often people learn to be prejudiced as they grow up.

You can be a prejudice fighter.

Remember the Girl Scout Promise and Law. You promise to be a sister to every Girl Scout and to show respect for yourself and others through your words and actions. Can you think of ways you can show respect for others through your words and actions? What would you do if:

- You heard a friend make a joke about people different from herself?
- Your classmate at school called someone bad names because of the way she looked?

- Someone told you that you couldn't do something you wanted to do because you are a girl?
- You saw a group of kids making fun of someone wearing clothes in an old style?

Think of some times you heard about people being treated unfairly. What could you do to be fair? Talk about how you can really get to know someone. How can you find out more about other people?

Leadership in Girl Scouting and Beyond

"I'm so bored! I wish there were more to do around here."

"Kathi, if you say that one more time," Reema threatened, "I'm going home! You know what, I *am* going home. All afternoon you've been no fun at all. I wanted to watch a video. I wanted to play with dolls. I wanted to play soccer. Every time, you said you didn't feel like it. Now you're bored. Forget it—I'm going home!"

Ruth looked at both of them. "We could go to the library and get some new books . . ."

"Who wants to read all day?" Kathi said.

Brownie Girl Scouts Make a Difference

"What do you think they're doing?" Reema asked.

"I don't know, but they look like they're having a lot of fun," Ruth said.

Kathi said, "I know who they are—they're Brownie Girl Scouts. Remember, there was a poster up at school in September. I didn't know that they did stuff like this."

"There's Zora and Ashley— they're in the class across the hall from us." Reema looked at the others and said, "I'm waiting until they're done and I'm going to talk to that lady in the front. I want to learn more about what they're doing."

"I spend so much time here," Ruth said. "We all do. And, I hate looking at dirt and garbage everywhere and we should help make this place better."

"What about you, Kathi? Will you stay?" Mie asked.

"All right. I don't want to walk home all by myself," she answered.

The lady was a Brownie Girl

"You don't sound very nice," Mie looked at Kathi. "It's a good idea. It's better than sitting around here. Let's go."

So, they went, though Kathi made a face and kicked at everything she passed all the way to the library.

Ruth ran up the steps. As the other girls followed her down the hallway to the children's books area, they heard all this noise coming from a group of girls in one of the meeting rooms.

Ruth poked her head in the door. The other three piled up behind her and peeked in. They saw all these girls around a table—some kneeling, some sitting, some standing, some hopping up and down— and all were helping a woman fill in a big poster.

Scout leader. Her name was Mrs. DeAngelo.

"What were all of you doing?" Mie asked. "It looked exciting."

Mrs. DeAngelo told them a little bit about how Brownie Girl Scouts make plans. She also told them about the kinds of service projects Brownie Girl Scouts do. The Brownie Girl

~ Do you see a problem in the community?
~ Library has lots of trash outside.
~ Lots of dirt-need grass.
~ Need extra trash cans.
~ No flowers or plants.
~ No bulletin board in entrance.
~ Children's books need labels.
~ Paint some shelves bright colors— put in children's section.
~ Get some information.
~ City is in charge of library yard.
~ Hours of the maintenance people were cut.
~ Brainstorm Actions.
~ Think carefully about the project.
~ Think carefully about each step of the project.
~ DO IT!
~ Think about what you accomplished.
~ Share what you have done with others.

Scouts in this troop had thought of many different problems in the community. They knew about people who were hungry and they had talked about collecting canned food and other ways to help hungry people. They knew that another Brownie Girl Scout troop was working on a community garden. They also saw that a local playground needed to be repaired, but after the girls had talked about all the different things they saw that their community needed, they decided to help the library where they had their meetings. They knew that lots of children loved using the library. Many older people spent the day there. And, so the Brownie Girl Scouts had thought of an Action Plan, a way to design a service project.

Mrs. DeAngelo also told them about all the other things that Brownie Girl Scouts do. They go on trips, sing songs, play special games, even do lots of different activities to earn patches called Try-Its, but, be-

ing a Girl Scout means doing service for your community and for other people.

TWO MONTHS LATER...

"Ruth, you look funny with dirt on your nose!" Kathi was laughing as she put another coat of green paint on the trash can.

"Maybe, but you have paint in your hair!" Ruth put some more dirt around the roots of the flower and looked at Kathi. "You don't say you're bored so much anymore."

"That's right," Reema said. "I haven't heard you say you're bored in a long time."

"That's because I'm not!" Kathi said. "I'm glad we're doing this service project for the library and I like all the stuff that Brownie Girl Scouts do. Becoming a Brownie Girl

Scout was a good idea! I guess I said I was bored too much. I was kind of rude to you. But, we weren't doing things like this before. I promise you won't hear me say it again—cross my heart!"

"Okay," Ruth said, "You want to stop working on this project and go to my house and watch TV?"

"No way," Kathi said. "We have lots more to do and TV would be too bor . . . . Ooops, sorry."

They were laughing so hard that they almost couldn't see how great the library looked. A new bulletin board hung in the entrance with a sign, "What's Going On?" along the top of it. Pink and red flowers marched all along the border of the building and two new trash cans painted bright green stood next to the library steps. Through the window, shelves painted blue and red and yellow and green held children's books. The library looked great and the girls felt proud and bursting with good feelings inside, because they were the ones who had done the work.

Getting Involved in Brownie Girl Scouts

When you became a Brownie Girl Scout, you learned the Girl Scout Promise. You promised to serve your country and to help people at all times. The girls in the story were making their promise come true. They were helping their community. All the people who used the library or even walked past the library would feel happier. When people work together in a community, they make life better for everyone. A service project is a task or plan for helping other people, improving the community, or improving the world beyond the community.

Citizenship

A citizen is a person who lives in a certain country and who has the special rights that country gives, such as voting, being protected by that country's army, and being able to live and work freely. You can also say that you are a citizen of a city or state or town. Good citizens are people who are active. They vote and they help their communities. If they see something wrong, they try to fix it. In what ways were the Brownie Girl Scouts in the story good citizens? Can you think of some things that your community needs?

_____

_____

_____

_____

_____

_____

_____

_____

_____

Doing a service project is one way to be a good citizen and to live by the Girl Scout Promise and Law. Service can be small. Reminding your friends not to litter is service. Recycling your aluminum cans and newspapers is service. Helping someone carry their packages home from the store is service. Service is catching! When you start doing things for other people, they often start doing things for others, too! If you keep your school playground clean, other kids won't be so quick to make it messy.

Action Plans

Do you remember the Action Plan from the story?

Do you remember the steps to doing a service project?

Here are the steps written on a chart. You can copy the chart onto your own paper when you are making plans or if you are doing more projects. You can also try doing a mini-service project at home. What can you do for your family? What can be done in your home? Take a look around and see what you can do!

Name of Project _____

What problems do you see in your neighborhood or community? Try these steps:

1. Name the problem. Then get some information. _____

   _____

2. Talk about actions and think of solutions.

   _____

   _____

   _____

   _____

3. Pick one that will work best.

   _____

4. Decide how to do the project.
   a. Think carefully about the project.

   _____

   b. What will be done?

   _____

c. Will it cost money?

_____

d. When will it be done?

_____

e. Is it too hard to do? Can we divide the project into smaller parts?

_____

f. Who will help us? Can we get other people in the community to help?

_____

g. How much time will we need?

_____

5. Do it!

6. Think about what we accomplished.

_____

_____

7. Share what we did with others.

_____

_____

Goal Setting

When you plan a project, you are setting a goal. A goal is something you want to achieve. You can set a personal goal—a goal for yourself—or you can set group goals. Many times in Brownie Girl Scouts you will set group goals. You may want to set goals to do service projects or citizenship tasks. As you grow, you will also set many personal goals. Learning how to roller-skate could be a goal. Keeping your room cleaner is a goal. Getting along better with your younger sister is also a goal. In many countries people set goals for themselves at the beginning of the year. These goals are called New Year's Resolutions. Lots of times these resolutions are too difficult to do, like lose lots of weight very quickly or get up one hour early every day and run five miles. Then, the resolutions are broken because they were too hard to do in the first place.

roller-skate. What would you do first? Maybe you would borrow some roller skates. Maybe you would buy some roller skates. Maybe you would talk to some people who roller-skate well.

What do you think you would do next?

Some goals are easier to achieve than others. "I will do better on my next spelling test" may mean you will study a little harder one night and not watch television. Some goals are easier for some people to do than for other people. Some people would find it easy to read one book a week. Other people may find that too hard to do. Each person has to set her own goals.

What goal would you like to achieve?

_____

_____

_____

Have you ever made a resolution that was too hard to keep?

When you want to make goals that you can do, you can make a plan. First, decide on your goal. Maybe you want to learn how to

What steps can you think of that will help you reach this goal? Make sure you write a time for each step to be completed.

_____

_____

_____

_____

How about a Brownie Girl Scout goal? What goal would you like to achieve in Brownie Girl Scouts this year?

_____

_____

_____

Leadership and Troop Government

Brownie Girl Scouts have many chances to be leaders. Taking part in a service project is a good opportunity to be a leader. You can contribute good ideas for doing the project. That is one kind of leadership. You can help people decide what they want to do. That's another kind of leadership. You can help people work together and cooperate. That's also leadership. You may be in charge of a group of girls—and that is leadership, too. There are many different ways to be a leader. Can you think of some others?

_____

_____

_____

_____

Brownie Girl Scout Ring

Round and round and round
   about
Take the hand of a Brownie
   Girl Scout!
Here we all are—
In a Brownie Girl Scout Ring—
Ready for almost anything!

In your Brownie Girl Scout troop or group, you may have a Brownie Girl Scout Ring. If your troop has lots of girls, or if you need to meet in smaller groups, you may also have circles. Both are ways to make plans and get things done in Girl Scouts. Both are ways that you can be a leader. A leader helps

other people decide and make plans—and do what the group has planned.

In a Brownie Girl Scout Ring, all the girls in the troop or group sit in a circle and talk about what they would like to do. Girls should take turns being the Brownie Girl Scout Ring "leader." The leader makes

Talking Signal

sure that everyone gets a chance to speak, that no one person does most of the talking, and that the discussion is orderly. Sometimes your troop leader may need to help you in the beginning, when you are first learning how to make plans in a Brownie Girl Scout Ring.

The "talking signal" is a good way to show that you want to say something when you are meeting in a Brownie Girl Scout Ring. If you make this sign, the leader knows who wants to say something. It's a lot easier than shouting!

When you are making plans in a Brownie Girl Scout Ring, you may need to make notes about your plans and you may need to collect and keep track of money. The girl who writes notes can be called a recorder or a secretary, and the girl who keeps track of money can be called a treasurer or money recorder. Sometimes, your troop leader may do these jobs in the beginning and give you a chance to practice them before you take turns doing them.

Brownie Girl Scout Circles

In Brownie Girl Scout circles, the troop or group is divided into small groups with five to eight girls in each circle. Circles are a lot like the patrols that older Girl Scouts have. Some circles last a long time and some a short time. Sometimes, you are a part of a circle that is doing a special job. For example, you may be a part of a circle that is responsible for making posters to advertise a recycled toy collection day. When this job is finished, the circle no longer meets. A circle may have a leader. Girls take turns being the leader.

A circle leader may have special duties. She may take attendance. She may make sure everyone in the group has her chance to speak. She may keep track of the kaper chart and be sure the group does the jobs they have been assigned. She may get something special to wear to show that she is the circle leader.

Leadership and Troop Money

You are also a leader when you make plans to earn money and spend money in your Brownie Girl Scout troop. Your Brownie Girl Scout troop or group gets money for activities in different ways—troop dues and money-earning projects like selling Girl Scout cookies. Sometimes you need more money because you want to do a special activity or trip. Then you need to earn some extra money. Decide how much money you will need. Make a plan. What if you want to go to the zoo? How will you get there and how much will it cost? Do you need to pay to get in? Will you need to buy lunch? Do you need money for extras, like souvenirs? Do you need to pay for people to come with you?

How does the treasurer keep track of the troop money? Here is a budget chart.

Date	Activity/Income	Add	Subtract	Sum

Here are some ideas for projects that will help you earn money. Can you think of some more?

- Try making printed notecards, stationery, and wrapping paper.
- Try washing cars.
- Try selling homegrown plants in decorated pots.
- Try fixing some old toys and selling them.
- Try making puppets, yarn dolls, knot bracelets, or jigsaw puzzles and selling them.
- Try baking loaves of bread and selling them.

- Try learning how to do some simple home repairs and offering to do them for your neighbors.
- Try making some of the crafts you learned about in the chapter "People Near and Far," and selling them.

Your leader can help you put your ideas into action. You might come up with many ideas. Decide on one as a group. Think of something that would be fun to do. You want to make money and have fun at the same time.

Girl Scout Cookies

Brownie Girl Scouts may decide to work on the Girl Scout cookie sale. You want to contribute to the activities of the group. Decide what part you can do best. You can sell cookies. Maybe you will want to sell cookies and help organize the money and the boxes. Maybe you will just help organize. All the girls and the leader can talk about what each person can do to help the troop.

Here are some ways to be a good salesperson:

- Learn about the cookies or whatever you are selling. How are the cookies special?
- Be able to tell the customer, the person who is buying, what you will do with the money. What special things do Girl Scouts do?
- Be able to tell the customer how much money she needs to pay, when you need to collect the money, and when she will get her cookies or other products.
- Make sure you give your customers the cookies and products on the day you promised.
- Always say thank you, even if a person decides not to buy anything. You are representing Girl Scouts and she'll remember that you had good manners.
- Practice what you will say and do before you see your first customer. Practice will make you a better salesperson.

- Be sure to know all the ways to be safe when you are selling things or doing other money-earning projects.
- After your group has earned money, make a report on how much money you have earned and what you will do with it.

Leadership and Group Planning

Leaders have special responsibilities. They do not always get to do what they want. They have to think about the members of the group. They have to find out the different ideas of the people in the group. They also have to encourage everyone to cooperate and to respect each other. They have to make sure that each person has a part in the activities. Sometimes that means letting other people do the things you wanted to do. Often it means letting other girls have the chance to be a leader.

In a Brownie Girl Scout Ring or in circles, you can use these four steps for planning things in a group. You can plan what service project you would like to do, what place you would like to visit, or which Try-It you would like to earn.

These steps will help you plan:

1. *Share your idea with others.* Speak up and let people know what you think. If you feel shy, practice what you want to say in your mind before you say it. Then, say it. Remember, there are often no "right" ideas—just a new way of looking at the same thing.

2. *Listen to others.* Listening to others is an important part of planning. Other people's ideas often help you think of some good ideas.

3. *Decide what you want to do as a group.* When you make group decisions, you should make sure that each person who wants to speak gets a chance and that only one person speaks at a time. No one should say anything that hurts someone's feelings. No one should keep talking too long. Everyone should have a say in the final decision.

4. *Look at the Action Plan chart on page 116.* Follow these steps. Having fun is also important when planning a project. Sometimes, things may not go the way you planned. Don't be upset if things aren't perfect. You can still learn a lot and still have fun.

Practice making decisions in a group. Practice deciding what steps you would need to plan.

What If . . .

- Your group decided to make the world more peaceful?
- Your group decided to help people get along better with each other?
- Your group decided to help others to have fun?
- Your group decided to help stop pollution?
- Your group decided to help every person have a place to live?
- Your group decided to stop all drug abuse?

These might seem to be very big things. But, thinking about what you can do and what your group can do may help make these very big things smaller. Each person has a lot of power to make things happen and to change things. Not only adults change things; kids can, too! What can you do to make things better for all the people who share this world with you? Where can you start? Look for the leader inside of you. She is there just waiting for you to give her a chance to make good things happen.

I am a leader because I _____

I am a leader because I _____

I am a leader because I _____

I am a leader because I _____

I am a leader because I _____

How and Why?

Kelsey's Computer Lesson

"I have a big problem. I have a super-duper kind of problem. And I don't know what to do." Kelsey had thought so much, her head felt like a giant water balloon ready to burst wide open. Her parents had just moved to Pittsford and she was the new girl in school. Kids were nice enough, but no one really paid her much attention, she thought. No one had invited her over yet. She really felt kind of invisible, so she did something really dumb. Her teacher, Mrs. Chee, had told the class that they were going to start writing stories on computers next week. All the kids thought that was great—computers were dynamite stuff. So, when Mrs. Chee asked who had worked on computers before, Kelsey's arm went right up in the air—she didn't even know she was waving her arm like a tree shaking in a hurricane until Mrs. Chee put her in charge of one of the computer learning groups.

And that is the problem. You see, the closest Kelsey had ever come to a computer was when her big sister, Denise, had taken her shopping at the mall and had told Kelsey she could type on the display computers while Denise looked at CD players! What was she going to do? All the kids in her group were depending on her. As they left school, they were all excited about next week. "Kelsey, I'm glad you're in my group," April had said. "My brother has a computer in his room and he won't let me touch it. Maybe once you show us how to use it, I can use my brother's and you can come over!"

As they were walking out the school door, Kelsey told the kids that she had to go back because she had left her sneakers in the classroom. Now, she sat, looking at the row of shiny computers. Slowly, her eyes got watery. She knew she was going to start crying.

"Hey! What are you still doing here?"

Kelsey jumped half out of her chair and turned around.

"What's wrong, Kelsey?" Rick Beckwith asked. Mr. Beckwith was the school custodian. He knew every kid's name. He was always smiling.

He always had a funny story. "Did something happen today in class? Are you feeling homesick?"

He looked so sympathetic and Kelsey felt so miserable, that she told him everything—how she had felt, what she had said, what the other kids had said, and what could she possibly do now? Everyone was going to laugh at her and think she was awful because she had lied and she'd never make any friends here.

"Well, Kelsey, you really did do something wrong. You should never pretend you know something that you really don't. You'll always be found out and you'll look really foolish. Worst of all, people won't trust you." He looked at Kelsey's face. "But, I think you know that. I use a computer every day. I keep track of all the school supplies. I do the budgets. I write letters and purchase orders. Would you like me to show you how to use this one? I think if we spent some time practicing, you'd know enough to get your group started. What do you say?"

Kelsey couldn't believe it. This was like a miracle! "Yes, please, I'd be really happy if you showed me. And, I know what I did was really wrong."

"Sure, but I have to tell the principal and you should tell Mrs. Chee before we get started— and your parents, too. Okay?"

"Okay, can we start tomorrow?" Kelsey replied.

Kelsey talked to her parents that night and to Mrs. Chee before school the next day. She said that she knew that pretending to know how to do something, especially when other people were depending on you, was wrong. And, after a lot of talking, her parents and Mrs. Chee said it was okay with them as long as Mr. Beckwith had the time.

(One week later)
Kelsey had finished showing the group how to save their stories on a disk. As they were leaving the school, April said, "You know, I thought you didn't want to be friends with anyone. You never smiled and you always seemed to want to do things by yourself. I'm glad you're in charge of this group. I'm glad we're friends. I think you're really nice. Let's go to my house and prac-tice on my brother's computer!" In the doorway, Kelsey saw Mr. Beckwith. He was smiling at her and gave her a long wink. She ran over and gave him a hug. "Thank you, thank you," she whispered. "You were my first true friend here."

The world is full of new things to learn. Think of all the new things you have learned in Brownie Girl Scouts. Can you write some of them here?

_____

_____

_____

_____

_____

Part of the fun of learning new things is learning how things work and why things happen. In this chapter, you will learn some of the hows and whys of things.

Brain Power

You use your brain to figure many things. You think about how much time it will take you to get home after school if you walk instead of taking the bus. You think about how long a piece of ribbon you will need for your hair. You decide if you will have enough time to do your homework and watch television. When you don't actually measure these things, but think and guess, you are estimating.

Try this estimation game. Think and guess:

How many words are on this page?

How many steps is it from the front of this room to the back?

How many windows are there in your school?

How many times does one of the people in this room smile?

What is the average size in inches of all the people's feet in this room?

How will you know if you are right? Make up some more estimation questions for your friends.

Besides estimating, brain power helps you do many things, like measure, work on a computer, tell time, and count.

Measuring

Different people in countries around the world found different ways to measure things. Some people measured distance using the length of their feet. Can you think of any problems that would happen if your foot was the only way you measured distance? Why do you think 12 inches are called one foot?

Today, most people use the metric system to measure, but in the United States, many people still use what is known as the English system of measurement. Many businesses, though, use the metric system.

Most rulers show the metric system and the English system. Do the following activities to practice measuring things with both the metric and English systems.

- Measure your height. How tall are you in inches? How tall are you in centimeters?
- Find a container that shows the amount in liters. Use the

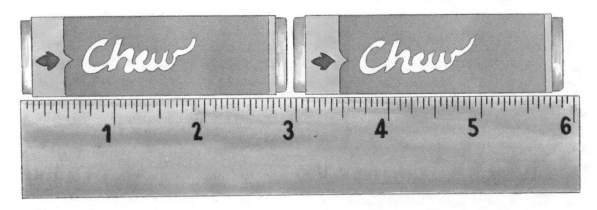

container to measure other liquids.

- Look through your groceries. Make a chart showing what something measures or weighs in the metric system compared to the English system.
- Try creating your own measurement system. How about using pieces of gum? Make your own gum ruler here. Now, how many gum sticks tall are you? If you don't want to use pieces of gum (or if you are chewing your ruler), try something else. What about peanuts or a favorite rock or seashell?

Computers

There are all kinds of computers. Some are very small and are used to make machines run better. Some very small computers are used in toys. Some are very big and keep track of millions of different things, like how much money is in the bank. Computers work very fast and use electricity. People make up instructions for computers. These instructions are called programs and tell computers what to do.

Each tiny instruction in a computer asks for a "yes" or "no" or "true" or "false" choice. You can get an idea about how a computer uses information to get an answer by playing the game "Twenty Ques-

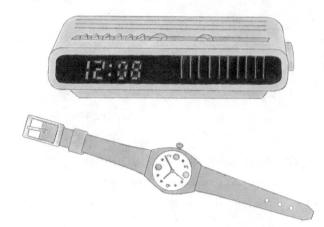

tions." This is an example of the choices a computer is given.

The game goes like this: Other people will try to guess what you are thinking. Think of something that is an animal (including people) or made of something that comes from animals (like leather shoes); something that is a vegetable (plants) or made of vegetable (like paper); or something that is mineral (almost everything else!). Others try to guess by asking questions that can be answered only with a "yes" or a "no." If you cannot answer the question with a "yes" or a "no," you should answer, "It does not compute," and the person who asked the question misses a turn.

Do you use a computer in school? Do you use a computer at home? in the library? Do you know someone who uses a computer at work? Find out about computers. Visit a place where they are used or sold and ask some questions. Practice using one yourself.

Telling Time

How long is a minute? 15 seconds? Can you tell without looking at a clock? With a buddy, get a watch or clock that has a second hand. When the buddy says "Start," close your eyes. Let her know when you think 15 seconds has passed. Take turns. Try 30 seconds and one minute. How good were you at estimating time? Now, try standing on one foot for 15 seconds. Can you do it?

How many times can you clap your hands in ten seconds? How many times can you stamp your foot in ten seconds? What other time challenges can you make up?

Hourglass

People have used different ways to tell time for thousands of years. One of the things people invented was an hourglass. Try making your own hourglass.

You will need:

- 2 one-liter clear plastic soda bottles with caps
- Heavy-duty package tape
- A nail

- Sand or table salt
- A clock

Follow this diagram to make your hourglass:

1. Fill one of the bottles with sand.

2. Use the nail to make a small hole in each bottle cap. Ask an adult to help you with this part.

3. Screw the caps on the bottles.

4. Put the bottle full of sand on the bottom and attach the empty bottle on top.

5. Turn the bottle over. Look at your clock. How long does it take for all the sand to move from the top bottle to the bottom bottle? How can you change the amount of time that your "Hour Bottle" tells? Try putting more or less sand in your hourglass. How does this change the time the hourglass tells? Think of some games you can play using your hourglass as a timer.

The Moon

Watching the moon can help you measure time. The moon is brightest and roundest about once a month. This is a "full moon." Find a calendar or check a newspaper that tells you the phases of the moon. The moon looks round for about three nights, so the second night is the night of the full moon. Mark the full moon on your calendar. Try to count the number of nights until the next quarter moon, half moon, full

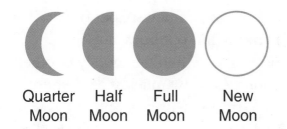

Quarter Moon   Half Moon   Full Moon   New Moon

moon, or new moon. Do you notice any other changes in the night sky when the moon is full?

Money

How is money measured? Pennies, nickels, dimes, quarters, one-dollar bills, five-dollar bills, and bigger bills are the kinds of money we use in the United States. Some other countries count their money in dollars, but only a few use dollars that look like United States dollars. Many countries have money that has its own special name and its own special look. Some countries have square coins. Some countries have coins with holes in them. Most countries have brightly colored bills with lots of pictures on them to make it easy to see the different amounts of bills that you have.

Look in a newspaper or visit a bank to find out how much one dollar is worth in the money of other countries. How much would your troop treasury money be worth in the currency of other countries?

Other Kinds of Money

Sometimes money doesn't look like money. Credit cards and checks are kinds of money people use to buy things without using coins or bills. If you put money in a bank account, you can use checks to pay for things with that money. You write the check. It is sent to the bank. The bank takes the money out of your checking account.

Credit cards can also be used like money. You use a credit card to charge what you want. The credit card company then sends you a bill once a month for all the things you have charged. If you do not pay the full amount, the credit card company adds extra money, called interest, to your bill. Credit cards can be more convenient (easy to use) than cash (bills and coins), but can also be more expensive.

Do you have a savings account? Some banks will let you open a savings account with an adult's permission. You can save money in a bank in a savings account. The bank will give you some extra money (interest), too, if you have a savings account. This is a good way to save money.

Talk to some adults about checks and credit cards. When do they use them? When do they use cash?

Visit a bank or credit union. What can you find out?

Science Is All Around You

Look around your world. Many of the things you see and many of the things you use every day depend on science and on technology.

Go on a science and technology hunt! Each of these things is an example of science or technology at work. How many can you find?

- Something made of plastic.
- Something made from oil.
- Something made from the forest.
- Something that moves in a circle.
- Something that comes from the earth.
- Something that uses a switch.
- Something made of metal.
- Something that uses electricity.
- Something that uses wheels.
- Something that measures.
- Something that uses metrics.
- Something made of glass.

- Something that makes or uses sound.
- Something from the ocean.
- Something made by people that can be recycled.
- Something run by computers.

Chemistry

Chemistry is the study of chemicals and how they mix and change.

Chemicals are all around you. Some may be right under your own kitchen sink or in your garden supplies. It is very important to handle certain chemicals with care. Some will react with others to make the air unbreathable, to burn your skin, or to poison you.

- Never handle chemicals unless an adult works with you.
- Don't touch any chemicals that say "Poison."
- If you have any doubt, always ask an adult whether a chemical is safe or not.
- Never mix household chemicals, like different cleaning solutions. This can be very dangerous.

One of the easiest places to learn about chemistry is in your own kitchen. When you make toast you are seeing chemistry in action. Heat is used to burn the bread and change it to toast.

Another chemical action that uses both heat and a combining of chemicals is bread making. You are using yeast to create air bubbles, and heat to make the yeast rise and bake the bread. Do the "Bread Making" activity in the Science in Action Try-It.

Matter: Solid, Liquid, Gas

Almost everything in the world is solid, liquid, or gas. Things can change from solid to liquid to gas. Water can be a liquid or a solid or a gas. What happens when water freezes into ice? It becomes a solid! And what happens when it boils and becomes steam? It becomes a gas.

- Try to find five things that are solid.
- Try to find five things that are liquid.
- What is air? The air you breathe is a gas.

Weird Glop

Make some weird glop. You will have something that isn't really a solid or a liquid.

You will need:
- 1/2 cup cornstarch
- 1/4 cup water
- Spoon
- Measuring cup
- Small pan

1. Pour the water into the pan.
2. Add the cornstarch a little at a time while stirring.

3. Keep mixing until your glop is one consistency. How is the glop different from water? How is it different from starch? Store the glop in a plastic bag. If it gets sticky, add a little starch. Do not eat the glop. What can you do with it? Try adding food coloring to make different colors of glop!

Dough Art

To create a chemical reaction, try the "Making Dough Shapes" activity in the Colors and Shapes Try-It.

Invisible Ink

You can make invisible ink from many different liquids. You cannot see what you write when you are writing, but when you heat the ink on the paper you can see your writing! You will need a cotton swab or paintbrush, paper, and at least one of the following liquids:

- Baking powder mixed with water
- Sugar mixed with water
- Lemon juice

 Write on paper with one or more of the liquids and then let it dry. Your message is now invisible. Place your paper between two sheets of scrap paper and heat the paper with an iron. Get an adult to help you with the iron. What happens? Try leaving your invisible ink message in a sunny, warm window. What happens?

Blow Up a Balloon

Blow up a balloon without using your own breath.

You will need:

- 1/4 cup vinegar
- Small plastic soda bottle (with a neck that you can place a balloon over)
- 2 tablespoons baking soda
- A small balloon

You will need several people working together.

1. Pour the vinegar into the plastic bottle.

2. Stretch the balloon mouth open and carefully pour the soda into the balloon.

3. Place the balloon mouth over the soda bottle, holding the balloon to the side so that the soda does not fall into the bottle.

4. When the balloon is tightly around the neck of the soda bottle, shake the balloon so that the soda falls into the bottle.

What happened? Can you figure out why?

Chemical Butterfly

A black felt-tip pen is made up of many different colors of chemicals. Mixed together, these colors look black. How can you see the different colors?

You will need:

- Black, water-soluble felt-tip pen (Try a variety of markers to see which works best.)
- Coffee filter
- Scissors
- Cup of water

1. Fold your filter in half and cut out a butterfly shape, like this.

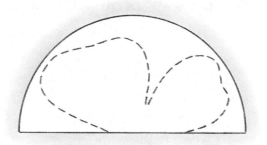

2. Run a heavy black line down the fold, like this.

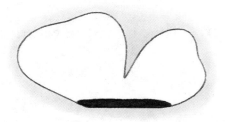

3. Dip the filter into the cup of water, like this.

Watch closely, but don't touch the filter. What happens?

Magnets

Magnets attract things made of iron. Go on a magnet hunt in your house. (Look at what else you can do on a magnet hunt in the Science Wonders Try-It.) How many things made of metal have iron in them?

Make Your Own Magnet

Make a temporary magnet by taking something that contains iron, like a pin or paper clip, and rubbing it in one direction many times across a magnet. Test your new magnet on another pin or paper clip.

Magnet Olympics

Have a Magnetic Olympics. Get a lot of different types and sizes of magnets and draw a line on a flat surface. Place different size objects at different distances away from the line to test which magnets are the strongest. See which magnet can hold the most paper clips. Make up some more Olympic events for your magnets and try to guess which magnets will be the winners.

Magnetic Attraction Box

You will need:

- Small cardboard or plastic box
- Steel wool
- Plastic wrap or a plastic lid for the box
- Magnet
- Tape

 **1.** Cut the steel wool into small pieces. Have an adult help you with this.

2. Put the pieces in the bottom of the box so they cover the bottom completely.

3. Place a piece of plastic wrap or a plastic lid over the box and tape it shut. Use the magnet to make patterns on the bottom of the box.

What kind of patterns can you make? How far away can you hold the magnet and still make the steel wool move?

Light and Color

All colors are made from three basic colors: red, yellow, and blue. These are called primary colors. How do you make other colors?

Making Colors

You will need:

- 4 flashlights
- Red, blue, yellow, and green balloons
- White wall, ceiling, or white sheet of paper
- Dark room

1. Cut the necks off the balloons.

2. Stretch the balloons across the flashlights.

3. Turn off the lights in the room.

4. Shine the red light onto the white surface.

5. Shine the blue light onto the red.

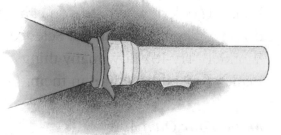

What happens? What color do you get?

Red plus blue =

Red plus yellow =

Yellow plus blue =

Combine the green with red, yellow, or blue. What happens when you shine all the colors together?

A Spectrum of Colors

The colors of a rainbow—red, orange, yellow, green, blue, and violet—are called the spectrum of colors. White light is made up of the spectrum of colors. A rainbow happens when sunlight, which looks white, is bent when it passes through raindrops. The bending light is a rainbow. On a sunny day, you can make your own spectrum of colors.

You will need:

- A straight-sided clear drinking glass
- A piece of card with a ½" (1 centimeter) slit cut into it (See drawing.)
- A sheet of white paper
- Tape

1. Fill the glass with water.

2. Tape the card to the glass. (See drawing.)

3. Put the white paper close to a window.

4. Put the glass on the paper.

What happens when the sunlight passes through the slit in the paper and the water in the glass?

Weather is the way the air is at a certain time in a certain place. The weather can change from day to day and from month to month. Look in the puzzle at right. Can you find the "weather" words?

S	U	N	F	R	O	S	T
N	P	M	R	A	W	Y	H
O	L	X	E	I	C	E	U
W	C	W	E	N	J	M	N
B	L	I	Z	Z	A	R	D
S	O	N	E	G	G	O	E
Q	U	D	N	H	O	T	R
A	D	L	O	C	F	S	Z

Answers: wind, cloud, cold, hot, fog, ice, snow, sun, blizzard, thunder, storm, frost, freeze, rain, warm

Sunny Days

The sun gives heat and light. It dries wet things and makes things grow. Sunlight helps your body make lots of Vitamin D, which your body needs to grow healthy bones and teeth. Sun can also be harmful to your skin. Have you ever gotten a sunburn? The sun was actually burning your skin! Even when you do not get sunburned, the sun can still hurt your skin. When you are in the sun, use sunblocks and sunscreens (lotion or cream that protects your skin from the sun). Don't forget to put more on after swimming or exercising. Can you think of some of the good things the sun does?

On a hot, sunny day, go outside and feel different objects in the sun and in the shade. Touch softly first to make sure you don't burn your hand. What kinds of things were hot? cold? warm? cool? Do the same with an outdoor thermometer. Measure the temperature in the sun, then in the shade to see the differ-ence. You can also look for things that get energy from the sun. What can you find that is solar-powered?

Evaporation

The heat from the sun can turn water into invisible water vapor in the air. (Water vapor is very, very tiny drops of water in the air.) Evaporation means that heat is making water vapor rise in the air. The water cycle means that water evaporates into the air and then comes back to the earth in raindrops. You can see evaporation happen by trying the following experiments:

- Put two tablespoons of water in a dish and place it in a very sunny spot. Put another dish with two tablespoons of water next to your first dish, but put a book or other type of shade between the sun and this dish so that it is not in the sun. Look at the dishes again in four to six hours. What happened?

- Fill a dark cup or glass half full of water. Stretch some plastic wrap tightly over the top. Put the cup where it is sunny and leave it alone. Look at it again in an hour. What happened?

Wind

Wind is moving air. The wind moves around the earth, bringing different kinds of weather with it. The wind blows and moves things in its path.

Look outside on a windy day. What is moving in the wind? Which things move most easily?

What kinds of things can you make that will move in the wind? Try the "Wind Wheels" activity in the Movers Try-It. Think of some ways to use wind power. What could you invent?

Clouds and Rain

Have you ever wondered what is inside a cloud? Clouds in the sky are made of water that is a gas. Fog is a cloud near the ground. Rain falls when the water mist in a cloud becomes drops that get bigger and heavier. What are some of the good things that rain does? Take a rain hike to see what changes are made by rain. Don't forget to dress properly.

Cloud Record

What can you notice about clouds? Try drawing the different shapes of clouds you see. What kind of weather followed what type of clouds? Do some kinds of clouds appear when it is rainy? Do some kinds of clouds appear when it is sunny? What patterns can you discover?

Rain Gauge

Make a rain gauge to see how much rain falls during a rainstorm. You will need a clear glass jar with straight sides or a clear plastic container with the top cut off. Place your gauge outdoors in a clear area before the rain falls. After the rain has stopped, hold a ruler to the side of your gauge. Measure the height of the water. How many inches fell? How does your measurement compare with the inches of rainfall reported in the newspaper or on television or radio?

Rain can also move the soil. Try the "Going, Going, Gone" activity in the Earth and Sky Try-It.

Frost and Snow

When misty water on the ground freezes during a cold night, you can see frost the next morning.

Water freezes when the temperature is below 32° Fahrenheit or 0° Celsius. In the morning on cold days, you can see frost on windows and leaves. If you look at frost closely, you can see the ice crystals.

Snowflakes are ice crystals. When it is very cold, the misty water in clouds forms ice crystals instead of water drops. When these drops get big and heavy, they fall and you see snow. Each snowflake (and there are millions and millions) is different—just like people! Not every part of the world is cold enough to get snow. If you live someplace where it snows, try this experiment.

Catch some snowflakes on a piece of dark paper or cloth that has been cooled to the temperature outside. Look at the flakes with a magnifying glass. What do you see?

Storms, Blizzards, Hurricanes, and Tornadoes: Weather to Watch

A storm has very strong winds. Hurricanes have winds that move at 73 miles per hour or more! Blizzards are strong winds and snow. Tornadoes are winds moving very fast in a tall funnel shape. Thunderstorms have lightning—the flash of electricity you see—and thunder—the noise you hear when lightning heats up the air so much that the air swells and almost explodes.

All storms can be dangerous. Strong winds can knock down power lines, trees, even buildings, and make very tall waves. Lightning is a very powerful burst of electricity in the sky. Thunder is the sound made when lightning flashes. Thunder can't hurt you but lightning can. It is very important to know how to stay safe in a lightning storm. Weather reports can tell you that bad weather is coming. You can sometimes see bad weather

(continued on page 142)

WEATHER WATCH
SCAVENGER HUNT

Go for a walk outside and look
for the things in this list.

- Something warmed by the sun.

  _____

- Something in the shade.

  _____

- Something blowing in the wind.

  _____

- A place that is cool.

  _____

- A place that is hot.

  _____

- A cloud that has a funny shape.

  _____

- Something that has been in the rain.

  _____

- Something that will protect you from the rain.

  _____

- Something that has changed color because of the

  weather. _____

- Something that has changed shape because of the

  weather. _____

(continued from page 140)

coming your way. You can tell when a thunderstorm is coming and how far away the storm is from you. When you hear thunder, count to five slowly and raise one finger. Then, count to five and raise the next finger. Keep counting in sets of five until you see the lightning. Each raised finger stands for one mile. If you have three fingers up, the lightning is three miles away.

Group Storm

Try making a "Group Storm." In a clear space, each person acts out one part of a storm—wind, thunder, lightning, clouds, rain, snow, hail, etc. Then, create a giant storm. How will each person's part be different as the "weather" changes?

Safety in Bad Weather

Thunderstorms

If you hear thunder or see dark clouds, you should follow these safety rules.

- Don't stand in an open field. Crouch down, don't lie down, on a sleeping bag or pile of clothes if you can. Try to put clothing or the bag between you and the ground.
- Don't stand under a tree. Lightning reaches for the tallest things to get to the ground. Lightning could hit the tree you are under!
- Get out of the water right away. Lightning can strike the water and hurt you.
- Stay out of ditches and arroyos. Storms can turn these ditches into big, fast rivers!
- Get inside a car or indoors. Once you are inside the car, do not touch the metal parts.
- If you are home, close all the windows.
- Don't use the telephone, air conditioner, television, or any other electrical appliance like a hairdryer.

Tornadoes

Tornado warnings are usually given on weather reports. If you hear that a tornado is expected where you live, you should follow these safety rules.

- Find shelter. The best places are storm shelters and basements, caves, tunnels, underground parking garages, or the inside hallways of buildings.
- Stay away from windows and outside doorways. Stay away from cars, trailers, tents, school gymnasiums, and auditoriums or stadiums.
- If you cannot find shelter, stay away from the tornado by moving to the side of its path or by lying flat in a ditch, culvert, or under a bridge. Put your arms over your head.

- Big storms can stop the electricity into your home, knock down power lines, or knock down big trees. See the section "Taking Care of Your Home" in the chapter "Taking Care of Yourself and Your Home" for tips on indoor safety during storms.

When the Storm Is Over

- Be careful where you walk after a storm. Electricity from power lines that have fallen can travel through water and wet ground. If you step in a puddle or on ground that is wet, you can get a big shock!
- Do not go near streams or river banks where water is moving quickly. Stay out of ditches and low areas.
- Do not walk on the beach or grass near the ocean. Big waves can move quickly after a storm and come right up onto the beach.

More About Lightning and Static Electricity

Lightning happens when static electricity builds up in clouds. Have you ever taken clothes out of the clothes dryer and discovered that they stick together? That's an example of static electricity. On a dry day, walk across a rug shuffling your feet in a dark room. Touch a door knob or other metal object. The spark you see is static electricity. This spark is like the lightning that jumps from cloud to cloud or from a cloud to the ground.

Another way to see static electricity is to tear some paper into tiny pieces. Run or rub a comb through your hair. Put the comb near the paper. What happens?

Static Antics

Try this activity to see how static electricity can make things move.

You will need:
- Tissue paper
- Silk handkerchief or small silk scarf
- Plastic pen
- Metal plate or tray

1. Cut a large circle out of the tissue paper.

2. Cut the circle into a spiral. (See drawing.)

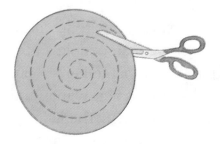

3. Put the tissue spiral on the metal plate.

4. Rub the plastic pen hard on the silk. If you don't have silk, rub the pen hard on your hair.

5. Hold the pen over the middle of the tissue spiral.

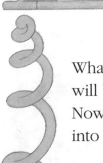

What happens? The paper will be pulled to the pen. Now keep lifting carefully into the air.

MY NATURAL ENVIRONMENT

What is your environment? Your world is more than people and buildings. Your natural environment is the air, land, water, plants, and animals around you. The living and nonliving parts are so connected that it is sometimes hard to separate them. To find out more about these connections, try the "Food Chain" activity in the Plants Try-It.

A mini-environment helps you understand something bigger by looking at something smaller. Get a string about two feet long. Go outdoors and find a grassy area to study.

Lay the string in a circle. The inside of your circle is your mini-environment. Study what is happening inside. Look through a magnifying glass. What do you see now? Make a list of what you see here.

_____

_____

_____

_____

Imagine how it would feel to be a part of this environment. Can you draw a picture or write about how it would feel?

Pollution

Everything you do affects your environment. Pollution describes what people do that changes or hurts the environment. Pollution can harm the air, water, soil, and living things.

Your everyday actions can cause pollution. Your litter can make a clean place ugly and can hurt animals who try to eat it. The gum that you throw on the ground can kill a small animal or bird who cannot digest such stuff. The fire in your fireplace might cause smoke in the air. Or you might pour something down a storm drain that goes into a river or lake and pollutes it. These are all types of pollution.

What are some things you can do to stop polluting? How can your actions as a pollution fighter help others in your family and your community?

Oil Spills

An oil spill is a bad kind of pollution that can happen when a pipe, container, boat, or truck carrying something harmful leaks. Sometimes the leak is caused by an accident. Sometimes people dump the chemical or oil into the ground or water. The chemical or oil goes into the water or ground and harms the environment. It can make the water too dirty to use for drinking water or swimming. It can kill the fish, plants, animals, birds, and even people who need the water or land in order to live.

Try making your own oil spill so you can see what oil does to clean water.

You will need:

- Ground red pepper or paprika
- Cooking oil
- Small bowl
- Clean water
- A tablespoon
- Small pieces of paper, fluff, feathers, dandelion puffs, apple seeds, or other small, light things
- Cotton balls or pads
- Ice cream sticks, small twigs, spatula
- Dish detergent

1. Mix the red pepper or paprika with three tablespoons of oil.

2. Pour this oil into the small bowl of clean water. What does the oil do?

3. Drop the paper, feathers, fluff, seeds, and other small items in the bowl, then take them out. What has happened to the things you put in the bowl? Water birds and animals can get their feathers, fur, or gills coated with oil. The oil can prevent them from keeping warm, flying, or breathing. They can die.

4. Try cleaning up your oil spill. Real cleanup crews try to blot up the oil with straw or other materials. Try using cotton balls or pads.

5. Cleanup crews also use booms or logs to keep the oil all in one place. Try using small sticks or a spatula. How much of the oil can you clean up using the cotton pads? Do the sticks help you clean up the oil?

6. Cleanup crews also add detergent to an oil spill. Add some dish detergent. What happens to the oil? But now you have added a new kind of pollution to the water! You can see that oil spills are very hard to clean up!

breathe. Planting trees helps fight air pollution. Participate in tree planting in your community.

Using a car less often also helps fight air pollution. Can you think of some ways to use a car less often?

Do the "Our Air" activity in the Earth and Sky Try-It to discover more about the air you breathe.

Do the "How Long Does It Take?" activity in the Earth Is Our Home Try-It to find out how long it takes for your garbage to go away.

The best thing to do about garbage is not to make it. That means you have to reuse it in some way, or recycle it or pre-cycle it. Pre-

Air Pollution

Air pollution is another kind of pollution that hurts all living things. Perhaps you know someone who has trouble breathing when the air is bad, or you have seen plants dying because of the lack of clean air. The automobile is the biggest air polluter in the country. Factories can also pollute the air.

There are several things you can do about air pollution. Trees are a natural air cleaner. Trees breathe in the air you cannot breathe, and release oxygen, the air that you can

Garbage: Reduce, Reuse, and Recycle

One of the biggest forms of pollution is garbage. There's just too much garbage! Where does garbage go? Many places have landfills—but they are getting full. Garbage does not go away once it is put in a landfill. You can burn it, which makes it smaller, but that often causes air pollution, and you still need a place for the ashes. You can bury it, and hope it rots away. But when you bury things, they usually don't go away because they need air in order to rot. So, some landfills have gotten so big that they look like giant mountains of garbage. Pheeew!!

cycling means buying the item that has the least amount of packaging or that is put into a container that is easy to recycle. For example, you can buy a hamburger wrapped in paper instead of a hamburger in a foam box. Choose a cereal in a box made from recycled cardboard. Buy a toy that doesn't have lots of extra plastic around it. Pre-cycling is smart!

Look for something that has too much packaging. Design a new package for it.

How do you know if something is made from recycled materials? Look for this sign:

Reduce. How much garbage does your family throw out every week? Keep track of a typical week's garbage. Can you think of ways to have less garbage? Try these with your family.

Reuse. Go on a recycling symbol scavenger hunt. See who can find the most items with a recycling symbol on them.

Reuse and recycle. Can you think of some things you can recycle or reuse at home? Wire hangers can often be returned to the dry cleaner to be reused. Funny papers can be used as wrapping paper or book covers. List ten things that you can recycle and do it.

_____

_____

_____

_____

_____

_____

_____

Conservation

There are some things that cannot be recycled forever and ever. Some resources, like water or land, have only a certain amount. They can be used up. To conserve something means to save it or use it only a little.

Clean water is an important resource. In some places in the world, people must move from their homes because they have run out of water, or they must travel far distances to get water. As a young girl in many places of the world, you would have the job of getting water for your family. You might walk three miles or more to the closest well or stream and then walk home with a bucket full of water on your head. In some places, you might have one bucket of water or less to last you the entire day. You would need this one bucket for washing, cleaning, cooking, drinking, and maybe even farming! Do you know how much water you use in one day?

Here are some ways you can save water. Can you think of some more?

- Don't run the water when you are brushing your teeth.
- Don't let the water run when you are scraping and scrubbing the dishes.

- Run the dishwasher only when it is full.
- Run the clothes washer only for full loads, or use

the water-saver cycle.
- Take shorter showers.
- Install a shower head that uses less water.

Saving Electricity

One important kind of energy is electricity. People use electricity in many different things at home and at work. It is important to conserve energy. Here are some ways that you can do this. Can you think of some more?

- Turn off the lights when you leave a room.
- Turn off the radio and television when no one is using them.
- Think of what you want in the refrigerator before you open the door. Then open and shut it quickly.

Go on an electric hunt in your house. List or cut out pictures of all the things you find that need elec-

tricity to operate. Are there any you could live without?

Make a poster that shows ways to save water and energy. Put it up in a place where people can see it.

Outdoor Skills and Adventures

Becky's Camping Trip

Becky woke up an hour earlier than usual on Monday. She listened for a moment, holding her breath. "Fantastic! No rain." She jumped out of bed, almost tripping over her bright red backpack and duffel bag.

"I just have to finish packing and I'll be ready to go. It's supposed to be about 80 degrees. So, I'll have to decide on my clothing and my other things to bring. Think I'll do this before breakfast."

Just then Becky's father knocked on the door, opened it a little, and put his head around the corner.

"How are you doing? Your first

overnight camping trip! Are you almost ready? Mrs. Williams said to meet at the First Baptist Church at noon."

"I don't think I have too much more to do, Dad," Becky said. "Just finish packing. I can't wait to go." "You mean you won't miss your dear old dad at all?" her father asked.

"We-e-elll," Becky said, "I guess I will—just a little bit, when we're not busy doing all our stuff at camp. Maybe I will be a little homesick, but Mrs. Williams told us to expect to feel homesick and she said we'll be so busy that we won't have too much time to think about it."

"Finish packing and I'll get you breakfast. What about my special pancakes for my special camper?"

"Great, Dad, I'll be downstairs soon."

Find out from your Brownie Girl Scout leader or older Girl Scout some of the things you can do on a camping trip. What things do you need to bring on a camping trip?

The outdoors is an especially good place for you to discover and observe the hows and whys of things in nature. Your outdoor adventure may be a nature walk, a picnic, an outside game, or a camping trip. Before you do anything in the outdoors, make sure you are ready. Always use this checklist to help you get ready.

☐ Plan ahead. Think about what

you will do. Talk about your plans with your friends, your parents, and the adults who will go with you.

☐ Learn skills. Learn and practice the skills you will need to enjoy the outdoors.

☐ Dress right. Make sure your clothes are right for the activities and the weather. Always be prepared!

☐ Keep safe. Learn the safety rules you need for the place you are going, and the safety rules for the equipment you will be using.

☐ Practice minimum impact in the outdoors. Leave a place better than when you found it. Be prepared to take out your garbage and practice conservation in the outdoors.

Look Out

What is it like where you are going? What do you need to know before going out? Here are some skills that will be important each time you go outdoors.

Plan Ahead

Your leader will help you plan where and when you go out. You will most likely work in your Brownie Girl Scout Ring to come up with ideas of where to go and what to do. Once you decide you are going out, you can discuss what you need to wear, what you need to take, and what will cost money. The best thing about most outdoor adventures is that they do not cost a lot of money. You only need to step out into your neighborhood, backyard, or schoolyard to enjoy the outdoors.

What to Wear

It is very important to learn about the best clothing to wear in different outdoor situations. It is always best to be prepared for the worst weather.

Some clothing hints:

- Remember that comfortable shoes and socks are a must for walking, whether in the city or the country. For long walks, always wear shoes that have been broken in.
  - On hot days, loose clothing is good because it lets you move freely and lets the air in and out. On cold days, it is important to wear layers of clothing to hold your body heat and keep you warm.
- Cotton and other natural materials are much better than other fabrics to wear, especially in the summer. Wool is a good material to wear in the winter, especially when layering. Wool has air spaces and will keep you warmer than cotton.

- Wear a hat with a brim in the sun.
- In very sunny weather, wear a lightweight, cotton, long-sleeved shirt to avoid sunburn. Never wear a sun top or halter on a hike in the sun.
- Wear a wool hat in cold, windy weather to help you keep your body heat.

- Wear wool socks and wool mittens or gloves in cold weather.

Try this experiment. Take a strip of cotton material and a strip of wool material about four inches long. (You can also do this experiment with wool and cotton socks.) Hold each over a bowl of water and let the bottom of the material just touch the water. What happens? What would happen if the material was the bottom of your pant leg? Which material would be better to wear in the snow or cold rain?

On a sunny day, put a piece of dark cotton clothing and white cotton clothing in the sun. After a little while, feel the clothing. Which is better to wear in hot weather?

A Day Pack

Do you carry a day pack to school? Day packs are useful for trips in the outdoors. If you plan on going outdoors for several hours, a whole day, or even several days, what are some things to carry in your day pack?

- A **water bottle.** You can use a plastic soda bottle and fill it with water from home, or you can buy a plastic water bottle. You need to drink water because you perspire, even on a cold day.
- A **whistle.** This is to use if you become lost or separated from the group. It's better to spend your energy blowing a whistle than yelling or crying. You should not blow your whistle unless you are lost or in trouble.
- A **rain poncho or windbreaker.** This is part of being prepared.
- A **quarter for the phone.** This is in case of an emergency. It is also important to have emergency phone numbers written down, along with your name and address.
- A **high-energy snack.** Some hard candy will work, or, try some gorp. (See page 154.)
- **Sunscreen** and **lip protection.** These will protect your skin and lips from the sun.
- A **sit-upon.** Make one before going outdoors. See the "Sit-Upon" activity in the Girl Scout Ways Try-It.

Minimum Impact

Minimum impact is an important way of living for Girl Scouts. You think about the way you affect your environment before you act, and because you think first, you do the least possible amount of damage to the environment. When you are in the outdoors, you try to leave it just the way you found it or help to make it better.

Some ways of practicing minimum impact are:

- Don't pick the flowers or plants that you see on a hike.
- Take a garbage bag to collect litter when your group goes on a hike.
- Pick up all the garbage and either take it to a trash can or carry it out.
- Don't waste water when you are outdoors.
- Don't wash out dishes near a lake or stream.
- Take your own cup, forks, knives, and spoons on outings, instead of using paper, polystyrene, or plastic materials.
- Don't feed wild animals in the parks or forest.
- When hiking, stay on the trails. If you do not, you can cause soil erosion.

Meet Out

Your first adventures might be in the backyard, playground, or in your neighborhood with your troop. There are lots of fun activities in your Brownie Girl Scout Try-Its to do in the outdoors. Many activities in other chapters of this book can be done in the outdoors.

Safety

Remember that you always go as buddies and that you are always prepared for the weather. If you need to go to the bathroom in a strange place, you should let an adult know and use her as a buddy.

Before you meet out, find out where the nearest drinking water is. If there is none, be sure your group takes a supply or you take a water bottle.

You probably will see animals in the outdoors. Some of them are pets. They may be on a leash, or they may be running loose. What should you do if you see a strange dog? Do the "Meeting an Animal" activity in the Animals Try-It.

What about the wild animals you see in the parks, like birds, or squirrels, or even rats? You should never approach a wild or strange animal. Animals may carry diseases

that you can get from being scratched or bitten.

It is important not to leave food lying around that attracts wild animals like squirrels, raccoons, rats, and even bears. These animals have food in their environment and will become pests if you feed them. You may feed birds in the winter because food is hard for them to find.

Use Your Senses in the Outdoors

The following activities help you use your senses of touch, sight, smell, and hearing to explore the outdoors.

- Try the "Touch, Smell, Listen" activity in the Outdoor Fun Try-It.
- Use a magnifying glass to find the smallest living things you can.
- Have a cloud watch. Look for clouds of different shapes and colors.
- Look for different shapes in natural things— circles, squares, triangles, ovals, diamonds, and straight lines.
- Look for different colors in the outdoors. Cut out ten different color patches from a magazine and try to match them in the outdoors.
- Go on a listening hike in the woods or by the water. Listen carefully. You may hear many different sounds. Can you identify the sources of the sounds you are hearing?
- Sit in a spot very quietly with a piece of paper and pencil. Put an "X" in the middle of the paper that shows where

153

you are. Listen for sounds and draw them on your map as you hear them. You can make symbols to show where the sound was, and how big a sound it was. Compare your map to the map of someone else listening at the same time. What was the loudest sound you heard? The softest? *Games for Girl Scouts* has many more outdoor games like this one.

- Learn many things through your sense of smell. Your nose can be a warning system for your body because things that smell bad might also be harmful. Smell as many different outdoor things as you can. Remember not to pick or cut any growing thing. Look for things already on the ground. Here are some ideas: a torn leaf, flowers, wet soil, a crushed blade of grass, recently snapped twigs, pond water, wet pieces of wood, pine cones, seashells, moss, evergreen needles.
- Go on a scent hike. Have a pair of girls or an adult lay out a simple scent trail that you can follow with your nose. Have them take an onion or cotton swabs dipped in oil of cloves or peppermint oil and rub it on things like trees or signs so that you can follow the trail with your nose.
- Try hugging a tree. How does your tree feel? How is it different from some other trees? Find out more about your tree. Try watching your tree throughout the year. What happens?
- Make a bark or leaf rubbing. Place a piece of paper over the bark of your tree, and with the side of a crayon rub in one direction to gently record your bark picture. Or use a leaf that has fallen on the ground. Place your leaf on a flat surface. With the paper over it, rub gently with a crayon to trace the outline of the leaf and its veins.

Move Out

Go beyond the backyard and playground to the neighborhood and nearby natural spots. Before you go, make some gorp to carry in your day pack. The ingredients are raisins, peanuts, dried cereal, dried fruit, dried coconut, and other dried nuts. Mix any and all of the ingredients and put them in a small container or plastic bag.

When you move out into the neighborhood and natural places, try these activities:

- Make a map of your neighborhood and do the "Street Safety" activity in the Safety Try-it.
- Learn to be a better observer in the outdoors. Practice describing the things you see and hear outdoors. Try this simple activity. Sit back-to-back with a friend. Pick up something or look at something and describe it carefully to your friend. Have your friend guess what you are describing.
- Make a record of a special spot. Take photographs, make a tape recording, draw a picture, or write a description. Share your special spot with others.

- Try a habitat hunt. Every plant and animal has a home or a place where it lives, called a "habitat." It may be a tree for a squirrel, the swamp for a frog, the forest for a deer, or the beach for a hermit crab. Look for a plant or animal in the outdoors. What things are part of its habitat? See how many animals you can find, and try to decide where each lives. Often a baby bird will fall out of the nest, or be hopping around on the ground waiting for the mother bird to come and feed it. It looks like it has been abandoned. What should you do? It is very important to leave the baby bird alone, so the parent can feed it. It is best to walk away.
- Try a seed hunt. Many plants start as seeds. Seeds differ in shapes and sizes and can travel, too! For example, dandelion seeds float as if they

Maple Seeds

Berries

Burrs

Dandelion

Violet Seeds

had parachutes. Maple seeds whirl like helicopter blades. Burrs ride piggyback on animals. Violet seeds pop like missiles. Berries are sometimes carried "air mail" by flying birds. Try to find as many different kinds of seeds as you can.

Explore Out

Plan a special outdoor activity. Learn some outdoor skills that will help you explore out beyond your neighborhood. You may still walk, take public transportation, or even car-pool to a special place. You will need some additional safety rules, and usually a permission slip from your parents.

Planning

When you begin planning, you may want to list some places to go. Have everyone list special places they would like to visit, or activities they would like to do. Your list might look like the one below.

PLACES TO GO:	THINGS TO DO:
The Mountains	Hike
The next town	Bike
An arboretum	Learn about trees
A forest	Plant trees
A national park	Visit with a ranger
The ocean	Study tide pools
An outdoor museum	Do a history walk
A lake resort	Swim
A pond	Study pond life
A stream	Clean up the stream

What other places would you like to visit? What other activities would you like to do?

Exploring out takes planning and preparation and you may spend meeting time making decisions about where you will be going, learning about the place you will be visiting, and practicing the skills you will need. Make sure you review the safety tips on page 153 and the sections on safety and first aid in the chapter "Taking Care of Yourself and Your Home."

Before You Go

Try making some no-cook snacks. Make a walking salad with carrots, celery sticks, raisins, and apple slices dipped in lemon juice. Stuff the celery sticks with peanut butter. Some other no-cook snacks that are good on a hike are cheese and crackers, fruit, energy bars, and dried fruit. If you are going to be traveling in hot weather, you should not take sandwiches with foods that can spoil. Peanut butter and jelly are two foods that won't spoil easily.

Before you explore out, learn how to make and use these trail signs:

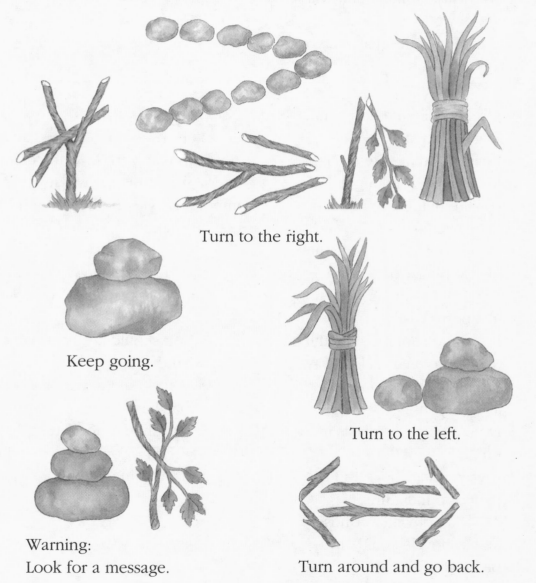

Turn to the right.

Keep going.

Turn to the left.

Warning:
Look for a message.

Turn around and go back.

You're Off!

Now that you're ready to explore out, try these activities:

- Lay a trail for another group. Hide a nice surprise at the end.
- Visit a pond or stream and find out what creatures live in this habitat. Build a "Water Snooper" to use in your pond exploration from the Water Everywhere Try-It.
- Explore the city. Do some outdoor exploration from the Building Art Try-It.
- Do some activities from the Outdoor Adventurer Try-It, such as "A Hike" or "Camp."

Sleep Out

After you have explored out and felt comfortable being away from home and in the outdoors, you will probably want to sleep out. You can get ready to sleep out in a camp cabin or tent by learning some new skills and going on a slumber party in someone's home or backyard. Sleeping out can be a lot of fun.

Staying overnight involves a lot of planning and learning some new skills. It is best to practice those skills in your meetings or when you are having your slumber party.

Fires

Campfires and cooking over a fire have always been a part of Girl Scout camping. Many people use cookstoves when they cook in the outdoors. To practice minimum impact, you should always have small fires. A fire that is too big uses too much wood and can get out of control.

You may be asked to help gather firewood. Look for small branches and sticks on the ground that have fallen from trees.

You may be asked to help start a fire. Your leader or an adult will show you how. There are some special fire safety rules that everyone needs to know.

- Always build the fire in a fire ring or fireplace.
- Never build the fire too large.
- Always tie back long hair if you are helping to build or cook over a fire.
- Never wear plastic or flammable clothing around a fire. Flammable clothing is clothing that burns easily.
- If you are cooking something over a fire on a stick, always be careful of the people around you.
- Do not play with sticks in the fire.
- Always wear shoes and long pants around a fire.
- A bucket of water or hose and a shovel should always be nearby.

Cooking

Your leader or a trained adult can help you learn how to cook over a fire or on a stove. It is very important to learn safety around the cooking area.

- You should never run or play around a stove or cooking area.
- You should always wash your hands.
- You should never play with matches.
- You should never turn the gas off or on unless an adult is watching you.

Read the section called "Eating Right" in the chapter "Taking Care of Yourself and Your Home." With a group or troop, plan what you will need to eat. You might decide to cook a simple one-pot meal over the stove or fire. Look at the food pyramid on page 39. What foods could you mix in a pot to make a delicious and healthy outdoor soup or stew?

You will need to learn how to tie a few knots in order to tie your sleeping bag and other camp gear.

An **overhand knot** is a knot in the end of a rope. This easy knot is made with one piece of rope. Follow the steps in the picture.

A **square knot** is used to tie two ropes together or to tie a package. It is also the knot used to tie a bandana around your neck.

1. Tie two pieces of rope together, following the steps in the picture. Remember this poem:
"Right over left and left over right Makes the knot neat and tidy and tight."

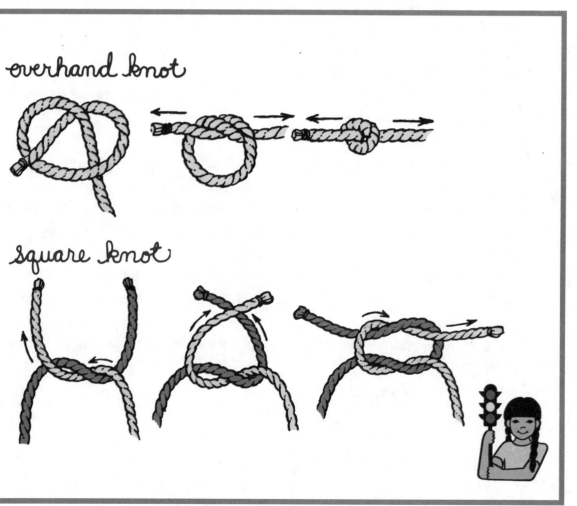

overhand knot

square knot

Sleeping

Before you sleep out:

- Find out about sleeping bags or bedrolls.
- Learn how to roll and tie a sleeping bag or bedroll.
- Have a sleeping bag rolling relay. You need two sleeping bags. The first person runs with the sleeping bag to a line that has been set. She unrolls the bag and runs back to tag the second person. That person must run up to the bag, roll it up, and bring it back to the next person in line, and so forth.
- Try sleeping at home in a sleeping bag or bedroll.
- Plan a slumber party at a friend's house or backyard.
- Participate in an overnight sponsored by your Girl Scout council.
- Plan an overnight at a council-owned campsite. Stay in cabins or wall tents that have cooking and restroom facilities.
- Find out about day camp or resident camp in your council. Plan to attend and practice your skills.

The outdoor skills you learn in Brownie Girl Scouts are just a beginning to many more adventures in the out-of-doors in Girl Scouting. You may live in a big city or in a small town. You may live on a farm or in a suburb. Wherever you live, you can find a way to use your outdoor skills and learn more about the outdoor world.

Brownie Girl Scout Try-Its
and Bridge to Junior Girl Scouts Patch

Sarah Joins the Troop

Veronica took her tray to the table and sat next to Nicki. Just then Jenny B. came over and sat across from them. The lunchroom was pretty noisy today—it sounded just like bees buzzing!

"I can't wait until our Brownie Girl Scout meeting this afternoon," said Jenny. "It's going to be fun getting ready for our camping trip this weekend."

"I know," replied Nicki. "My family goes camping all the time, but this will be my first time with our troop. I hope Mrs. Pinski lets us tell stories. My family always does that when we go camping!"

Veronica had never been camping before and wasn't even sure she would like it. But her Brownie Girl Scout leader, Mrs. Pinski, was really cool, and always helped them learn neat things. Everyone in the troop was really excited about the camping trip.

Just then, Sarah, a new girl in school, came and sat at their table. She was wearing her Brownie Girl Scout uniform. Nicki had heard Sarah was going to join their troop.

"We were just talking about our camping trip this weekend. Are you going?" asked Nicki.

"Yes, I think so," said Sarah. "I asked my mom and she said yes."

"I've never been camping before," said Veronica. "Mrs. Pinski has been teaching us lots of things to get us ready. Last week we practiced making a bedroll. Today we're going to use our mess kits and go over the safety rules again."

"Is there a Try-It for camping?" Sarah asked.

Jenny answered, "I don't really know. We don't do a lot of Try-Its in our troop"

"In my other Brownie troop, we got a lot of Try-Its," Sarah said

as she pointed to her sash.

Nicki got excited. "I remember! Mrs. Pinski said we would do some Try-It activities this weekend. But we're going to do lots of other things, too." Veronica also remembered. "We already did some other stuff for Try-Its, but we haven't finished everything yet. When we do, we'll have a special ceremony."

"Really?" Sarah said, "We got our Try-Its when we finished the activities. A special ceremony sounds like fun. What do you do?"

"A ceremony is like a special celebration. We had one when the other new girls joined our troop.

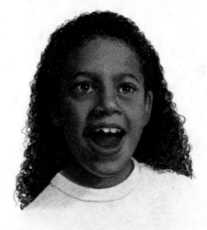

We took turns saying poems and we sang songs like 'Make New Friends.' Some of us are working on a special flag ceremony for our camping trip this weekend."

Sarah looked interested. "What else do you do?"

"We do lots of fun stuff all the time," said Veronica. "Last week we went to the Natural History Museum and saw dinosaur skeletons. It was fun!"

"Another time we planted flowers and plants in front of the nursing home," said Jenny B. "Then we had a party with the people who live there. We had a great time!"

Make New Friends
(Four-part Round)

Moderato

U.S.A.

1. Make new friends but keep the old;___
A - mis - tad es lo - que nos u - ne.

3. One is sil - ver and the oth - er gold.
Y lo que nos ha - ce pro - gre - sar.

Atención: Un error muy común es dejar fuera la nota alta en el tercer compás. Esto resta brillantéz a la ronda.

Beware: A common mistake is to leave out the top note (E♭) in bar 3. This takes away the brightness of the round.

© From "The Ditty Bag" by Janet E. Tobitt. Reprinted with permission.

"You know what I liked?" asked Nicki. "The time we had that spaghetti dinner for our families. We decided how much money we had to spend and then we shopped and then we cooked the whole dinner ourselves!"

"That sounds like fun, too!" Sarah said. "I like cooking. In our troop, we earned the Good Food Try-It. I even taught my mom some stuff about eating healthy food."

Sarah thought for a minute. "You really do a lot of fun things, trips, and projects. I thought getting a lot of Try-Its was fun and they are fun to do, but trips and other stuff you were talking about sound like fun, too!"

Just then the bell rang. Veronica, Nicki, Jenny, and Sarah all got up from the table.

"I think we'll have a lot of fun on our camping trip," said Sarah. "We sure will, even Veronica!" the others all said at once.

About Try-Its

Brownie Girl Scout Try-Its are just one part of the whole Girl Scout program. Their name says it all—Try-It. You don't have to be perfect at an activity; you just have to try. Sometimes you may decide you don't want to finish a Try-It. That's okay. You can come back to it later. Or you can just go on to something else. You will want to do most of the activities with your troop or group anyway, and lots of things are more fun if you do them with others. The only requirement for Brownie Girl Scout activities is that they be fun!

You will probably work on Try-It activities as a group. Your whole troop or group may work together, or maybe just the girls in your Brownie Girl Scout circle. Before you start a Try-It, look at the section "Leadership and Group Planning" in the chapter "Leadership in Girl Scouting and Beyond" and read about working in a Brownie Girl Scout Ring or circle. Be sure to use the four steps as a guide to making decisions as a group.

For each Try-It, you have six activities to choose from. When you have finished four activities in one Try-It, you have done enough to complete it. You and the other girls can then plan a Court of Awards ceremony as a special way to receive your Try-Its. Sometimes you'll have one Court of Awards a year or you may have Court of Awards more often. Each troop is different.

Some of the Try-Its have a "More to Try" section. This section is extra and can be done if you really like a topic and want to learn more about it. You can also do more than four activities in a Try-It.

As Mrs. Pinski and the girls in her troop already know, Brownie Girl Scout Try-Its are a part of what you can look forward to as a Brownie Girl Scout. You don't have to earn all 40 Try-Its. In fact, if you do, you're missing out on a lot of the other things you could be doing, like camping or community service projects. And doing something just because it's fun!

HERE IS A LIST OF THE BROWNIE GIRL SCOUT TRY-ITS:

A
Animals
Around the World
Art to Wear

B
Building Art

C
Careers
Caring and Sharing
Citizen Near and Far
Colors and Shapes
Creative Composing

D
Dancercize

E
Earth and Sky
Earth Is Our Home

F
Food Fun

G
Girl Scout Ways
Good Food

H
Her Story
Hobbies

L
Listening to the Past

M
Manners
Math Fun
Me and My Shadow
Movers
Music
My Body

N
Numbers and Shapes

O
Outdoor Adventurer
Outdoor Fun
Outdoor Happenings

P
People of the World
Plants
Play
Puppets, Dolls, and Plays

S
Safety
Science in Action
Science Wonders
Senses
Sounds of Music
Space Explorer
Sports and Games

W
Water Everywhere

ANIMALS

There are many different kinds of animals. Insects, snakes, lizards, frogs, fish and snails, dogs, cats, and cows are animals. Explore the world of animals in this Try-It.

Meeting an Animal

How should you behave when meeting an animal for the first time? It depends upon whether it is someone's pet or an animal in the wild. Read about meeting an animal on page 153 in "How and Why?"

Visit a veterinarian or animal shelter and learn about the differences between animals that are pets and animals that are wild. Find out what the rules of conduct are around such animals. Find out what dangers there are in approaching wild or pet animals. Make a poster or play about how to treat animals in the neighborhood or in the wild.

How They Look

Animals are divided into groups by the kinds of bodies they have and how they live. Can you find animals that match the descriptions below by observing them in your habitat, at the zoo, or in a book?

- Animals that have 2 legs, 4 legs, 6 legs, and 8 legs.
- Animals with no legs.
- Animals that have fur.
- Animals that have lips.
- Animals that live in water.
- Animals that have antennae.
- Animals that have soft, squishy bodies.
- Animals with feathers.
- Animals with wings but no feathers.
- Animals with scales.
- Animals that have shells.
- Animals with paws, animals with claws, animals with flippers, animals with hooves.

How They Act

Observe animals at the zoo, in your neighborhood, or on TV. Find out how animals act. Find animals that:

- Eat meat.
- Dig.
- Fly.
- Hop.
- Crawl.
- Live underground.
- Live up in trees.
- Swim.
- Run.
- Live in groups.
- Live alone.
- Travel long distances.
- Stay close to home.

How can you keep a record of this information?

How does the type of bodies that animals have affect the way animals act?

Shelter for All

Every animal needs some sort of shelter to protect it from the weather and other animals. The place where a plant or animal lives is called its habitat. It includes space, food, shelter, and a place to raise young. Do the habitat hunt on page 155 of this book.

Animal Sounds

Animals communicate in many different ways. Some touch; some make noise; and some leave a smell. Play animal sounds charade. Have your friends guess what animal you are. Here are some animals to try.

Chicken	Lion	Parrot
Bee	Frog	Skunk
Cricket	Alligator	Elephant
Monkey	Horse	Donkey
Rattlesnake	Whale	Lizard
Cat	Squirrel	Robin
Dog	Fly	Bat

Write the name of each animal on a small piece of paper. Put the pieces of paper in a bag and shake well. Pull out an animal name and show others who you are by sounding like that animal.

Animals in Danger

Many animals need a special habitat to survive. Survival means that an animal can live and raise its young, while also having enough food, water, space, and shelter. When an animal group, called a species, loses animals because there is not enough food, water, space, or shelter, the animal species is said to be endangered. The group of animals can die if there are not enough of them to have families. Once a species disappears, it is extinct. Find out about an animal species that is endangered in your state or area. Find out what people are doing to save it and why. What can you do to help?

AROUND THE WORLD

The world is made up of many different peoples and cultures.

Brownie Girl Scouts Around the World

Look back at the chapter "People Near and Far." What did you learn about Brownie Girl Scouts in Ghana, Thailand, Peru, and Denmark? Pick one of the activities on these pages and do it. You could make Adinkra cloth or a kite or a woven belt or learn a game.

Look at the World

Here is a fun way to learn about the world.

1. Find the United States of America on a map or globe. Try to use one that is new. Names of countries change often.

2. Look at the other countries on the map or globe. Name two countries close to the United States and two countries far away.

3. The equator is an imaginary line around the world that is an equal distance from the North Pole and the South Pole. The countries farthest from the equator have a very cold climate. Find the equator and follow it around the world on a map or globe.

4. Name ten countries that you think would have a hot climate.

5. Name ten countries that you think would have a cold climate.

Books

Many storybooks have been written about families from different countries. Visit a public library and ask the librarian to help you find a story about a family from another country. Read the story to a younger child (maybe a brother or sister), or have someone read it to you.

Global Family Card Game

Make a global family card game. Collect pictures of people from different countries. Make sure your pictures show people as they really live and dress. Don't use old pictures that may be out-of-date or inaccurate.

You will need:

- Magazines and newspapers (your public library may give you magazines it no longer needs)
- Glue
- Scissors
- Index cards or light cardboard cut into 3″ x 5″ shapes

Glue a picture onto one side of your card. Write the name of the country on the back of the card. Make up some games using your global family cards.

More to Try: Hang your cards from wire hangers/wood dowling and make a mobile.

Troop Recipe Book

Many foods you like to eat come from another country. Have you ever had noodles, tortillas, egg rolls, peanut butter, or quiche? Where did they come from? Many foods also were first eaten here. Did you know that American Indians grew the first tomatoes, then shared them with the rest of the world?

You can find out more information like this by making a "Troop Recipe Book." Bring in family recipes. Share information about your recipe. Where is it from? Who gave it to you? How do you make it? Put the recipes together in a book. Why not try them for a special lunch or supper?

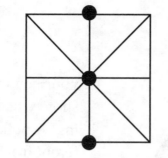
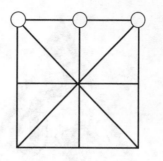
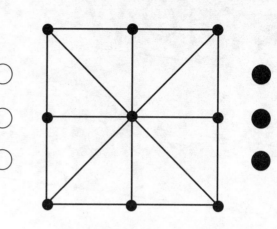

Tapatan

In countries all over the world, children play a game much like our tic-tac-toe. The game has other names. In England it is called Noughts and Crosses. In Sweden it is Tripp Trapp Trull. In Austria it is Ecke, Necke, Stecke. And in the Philippines it is called Tapatan. Like tic-tac-toe, the object is always to get "three in a row." Have fun playing Tapatan.

Each player needs three moving pieces. They can be pebbles, buttons, or checkers. Use the pictures to help you play.

1. Draw this diagram on paper or cardboard.

2. The game is played on the nine points where the lines meet. Players take turns putting their pieces on an empty point. This continues until all three pieces of each player are placed on the game board.

3. Player one moves one piece along a line to the next empty point. The pieces can be moved up or down or diagonally. Jumping over the pieces is not allowed. Player two does the same and they continue to take turns.

To win, a player must make a row of three across, up and down, or diagonally. If neither player can get three in a row, the game is called a draw.

TRY IT!
ART TO WEAR

Art can be many different things. It can be a painting or music or a poem. You can even wear works of art. Try these activities to see how.

T-Shirt Art

Show others your art by wearing it! Turn a plain T-shirt or sweatshirt into your own work of art.

You will need:

- A plain T-shirt or sweatshirt
- Paper
- A pencil
- Crayons or fabric paint

Decide what size design will fit on your shirt and draw it on a piece of paper. When you are satisfied with your design or picture sketch, you are ready to copy it onto the T-shirt. If you use paint, follow the directions that come with it. If you use crayons, color your design on a piece of white paper. Then put the design face down on the place where you want it. Put a paper towel on top. With the help of an adult, iron over the design. You may have to press down hard. It will soon show up on the shirt. Have a fashion show with the shirts you and your troop make.

OR

Hats can do more than keep your head warm. They can also show what a person does for a living. A police officer's hat looks different from a baseball player's cap. Sometimes people wear hats, like party hats, when they're celebrating. Make a special hat for yourself. Create your hat from paper, or find an old hat at home or in a secondhand store. You can also sew a hat from scraps of fabric. Decorate it with colored paper, fabric scraps, yarn, sequins, buttons, or natural materials.

Face Paint

Have a face-painting party. Make certain an adult is present. Be sure to use makeup and paints that are made just for the face. If you can't find enough face paint, or you just want to try something new, here are some face paints you can make right in your kitchen!

You will need:

- White shortening (or cold cream)
- Cornstarch (or baby powder)
- Unsweetened cocoa
- Food coloring
- Spoons
- Small bowls
- Cotton swabs to apply face paint

1. Mix the shortening and cornstarch together until they are creamy. Put some in each of the bowls.

2. Add the cocoa and more shortening to some bowls to make darker skin colors and shading.

3. Add food coloring to the rest of the bowls. Experiment with the colors.

4. Start painting each other's faces. Try different patterns, designs, and colors.

5. Clean up when you are

done. Use plenty of water on your face and don't rub hard with towels.

If possible, invite a makeup artist to your troop to demonstrate different kinds of face painting.

Papier-Mâché

Papier-mâché is a light material made from wastepaper and glue that can be easily molded. This is an easy way to make a new bracelet. It's lots of fun but really messy! Be sure to cover your clothes and your work surface.

You will need:

- A cardboard tube that fits loosely over your wrist.
- Scrap paper for strips.
- Colored tissue paper, also used for strips.
- Scissors.
- Flour and water paste or liquid starch.
- A shallow pan (like the ones pies come in).

1. Cut the cardboard tube to the width you want for your bracelet.

2. Tear or cut the scrap paper and the tissue paper into strips. If you are doing this as a group, you can all do this at once.

3. Mix up a paste in the pan using flour and water. Make sure it is thin and runny without any lumps. Or, instead of flour and water, you can pour liquid starch in the pan and use it for paste.

4. Dip the scrap paper strips

into your paste, and pull them out one at a time. Layer the strips around the cardboard tube bracelet. Create an even surface or one with patterns and bumps. Use your fingers to mold and shape.

5. For the last layers, use strips of colored tissue paper. Create patterns or a solid surface. Place the bracelet in a warm, dry place. The thicker your bracelet is, the longer it will take to dry. Liquid starch may take longer to dry also.

Mask Making

Many people around the world make masks for ceremonies, holidays, or dramatic events. Some masks are used to tell stories. Choose a holiday or special event and make a mask. Use a paper bag to create a new personality. Add bits of paper, yarn, or other materials to a paper bag. You can also draw on the bag with crayons or paint. Or use heavy cardboard as a base to create a mask that you hold to your face by a handle. (Chopsticks, popsicle sticks, or pencils make good handles.)

Beads

Create your own beads that you can use to make jewelry.

1. Follow the instructions for making the dough on page 186. You will need toothpicks to make the holes in the beads.

2. Take pieces of dough about the size of a grape, and roll or press them into beads with different sizes and shapes.

3. Use the toothpick to make the hole in the beads.

4. Let the beads dry. You can put them on string to make necklaces and bracelets.

More to Try: Decorate your beads with colored paints.

Knots

You can tie knots to make bracelets, necklaces, belts, and other things. On page 159 are some easy knots to tie. Find different kinds of string, ribbon, ropes, and cords. Look for a lot of colors.

Tie square knots until you have the right length. Then tie overhand knots at the end of each piece of rope.

More to Try: Try the finger-weaving activity on page 96. Make a belt, bracelet, or other things to wear.

TRY IT!
BUILDING ART

An architect (ar-ki-tekt) is someone who designs buildings and other spaces. You can have fun learning about architecture by doing this Try-It.

Your Home

Read pages 44–46 in "Taking Care of Yourself and Your Home." Learn how to do some of the things on the list.

Looking at Buildings and Spaces

Look at as many buildings as you can in one day. Look for different shapes, patterns, designs, sizes, colors, and materials. Look at play areas and how they are designed. Are the buildings and other spaces good for the people and other living things that use them? Share your ideas with another person.

The Best Neighborhood

Think of a neighborhood that would be a place where you would really like to live. Get a piece of cardboard or heavy paper at least 36 inches x 24 inches in measurement. Using that as a base, glue or paste cut-out pictures you find in old magazines that could go in your ideal neighborhood. Get crayons, markers, or paint to draw in other parts of your neighborhood that you think should be included. Show your ideal neighborhood to others and explain not only what it looks like, but how you would feel in your neighborhood, how people would act in it, what you could do there that you can't do in your neighborhood now.

Discovering the Strengths of Shapes

Architects have to know how strong building materials are and how different shapes can hold weight. Experiment with the strengths of designs and shapes by following these steps.

You will need:

- Paper
- A small stone or a coin or a button

1. Sit on the floor. Take a single sheet of paper. Hold it by one edge in the air so the paper sticks out straight over the floor. Next, take a small stone, coin, or button and place it on the paper. (See the picture.) What happens? The flat piece of paper should be too thin and weak to hold up the stone, coin, or button. It does not have enough strength to hold the object.

2. Next, take that same piece of paper and fold it in quarters like a book. (See the picture.) Try to rest the stone, coin, or button on the edges of the paper. What happens? By changing the shape of the paper, there is more strength and the paper can hold up the object.

3. Make the fan shape and the curved shape out of your paper as in the picture and try to balance the objects on the paper. What happens? They should be able to support the objects.

4. Experiment with other curved and folded shapes to see which ones can hold up the stone, coin, or button. Make a design sculpture with your shapes. Glue or tape may help put the shapes together. You can also make slits in the paper and fit the pieces together.

More to Try: Do this with friends. Using only tape, paper, and scissors, make a model of a house, a store, or some other kind of building. Make a bridge, too.

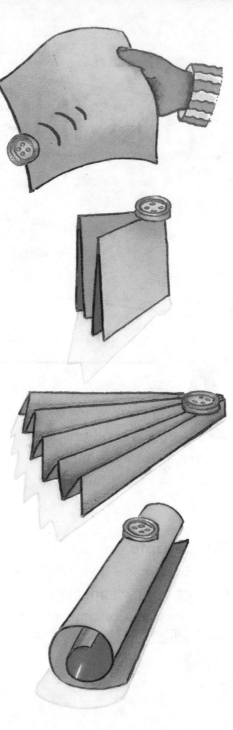

DESIGNING AN IDEAL GIRL SCOUT MEETING PLACE

Think about all the things you do and would do at your Girl Scout meeting place. Then imagine the perfect Girl Scout meeting place. Draw a picture or sketch or make a model that you can show others.

SCALE:	APPROVED BY	DRAWN BY
DATE:		
		DRAWING NUMBER

Designing Space for Someone with Special Needs

Read about people with disabilities on pages 75–79. Think about where you live or where you go to school. What would you change about those places to make them safer and more accessible (easy to get at, easy to get around in) for someone with a disability? Here are some ideas. You might make the doorways and halls wider. You could make a light flash when the telephone rings. You could make sure nothing is on the ground that could cause someone to trip. What else could you do? How could these ideas help someone with a disability? How could they also help someone without a disability?

TRY IT!
CAREERS

Future Jobs

Many jobs that people have today did not even exist many years ago. Interview some adults and ask what they wanted to grow up to be when they were young. Think about how the world will be when you are older. Make a list of the new kinds of jobs you think will be available when you grow up that don't exist now.

Today girls can look forward to more career choices than ever before. Have you thought about what you would like to do when you grow up?

Autobiography

Write or tape an autobiography. That's the story of your life. Find a book with blank pages, or make one of your own or use a cassette or videotape. Look at the time line you made on page 38 for some ideas. What else can you add?

What Am I Good At?

Read pages 66–67 about careers in "Taking Care of Yourself and Your Home." Some careers have more men in them than women. Find out about one of those careers. Try to interview a woman who is working in a career that more men used to do than women. What questions could you ask her?

Women Pioneers

Find out about famous women inventors or explorers. What were some of the things they did? Can you find women who were pioneers in other jobs? Share what you learn with your troop or group.

Career Charades

Divide the troop or group into two teams. Each team should take turns having a girl act out one of the jobs listed below. The other team has to guess what she is. You can also make up your own list or add to this list.

Bank teller

Coach

Youth counselor

Physical therapist

Book illustrator

Scientist

Bus driver

Pharmacist

Veterinarian

Musician

Photographer

Plumber

Astronaut

Lifeguard

Potter

Chef

Farmer

TV reporter

Learn to Earn

Learning how to handle money is important now and for when you get older. Read about money and budgets on page 121. With a group, plan one of the money-earning projects.

More to Try: You can learn business skills in your Girl Scout activities. There are tips on selling cookies on page 122. If you participate in this type of activity, practice these ideas.

TRY IT!

CARING AND SHARING

No one in the world is exactly like you—or your friends! Show how you care about yourself and others with these activities.

I Care

Be a "secret pal" to someone. Think of nice things you can do for your secret pal. You may want to write a poem, make a friendship pin, send a card, or be a helper. Think of other things you can do.

Favorites

Everyone has some things that they like better than others. Make a list of some of your favorites—school subjects, books, places, things to do. Compare your list with your friends' lists. What things are the same? different? How much influence do your friends have on what you like? What about your family?

What If?

With your troop or group, talk about what makes a person a good friend. How can you be a good friend to another person? With your Brownie Girl Scout friends, role-play what you would do for each of these events.

- Your best friend is crying and you want to show you care.
- One of the girls in the troop has a birthday.
- Your mother has to finish a big project for work the next day.
- A neighbor falls and breaks her leg.
- Your friend is afraid she will fail a test.
- A classmate forgot her lunch.

You may want to think of other scenes to act out.

180 TRY IT•TRY IT•TRY IT•TRY IT•TRY IT•TRY IT•TRY IT•TRY IT•TRY IT•TRY IT•TRY IT•TRY IT•TRY IT•TRY IT•TRY IT

Feelings

What do you think of yourself? What do other people think of you? Do at least two of these activities.

- Write a story about your best friend. What do you like best about her?
- Write a story about one time when you were very happy.
- Draw or write about one time when you were very scared.
- Draw or write about one time you solved a problem that no one else could.
- Draw or write about one time when you were very mad.
- Draw or write about a time when you were very brave.
- Ask someone to draw a picture about what they think is best about you.

Differences Are Okay

Many people look different from you. Some have skin or hair that is another color. Some are taller or shorter. One person may see better and another not hear as well. All these people have similar feelings on the inside. They also have talents to share.

With your Girl Scout group, find out about ways that you are different from each other. Choose a partner and stand or sit facing her.

Write down three ways your partner is different from you. Write three ways you are the same. Change partners and do the same thing. Come together as a group and talk about some of the ways you are different and the same. Are these differences important?

A Friend's Scrapbook

Make a scrapbook that tells about all of your friends.

You will need:

- Construction paper
- Writing paper
- A stapler
- Markers or crayons
- A pencil

1. Fold the construction paper in half. This will be the cover.

2. Decide how many friends you want to put in your book. Make a page for each of them.

3. Staple the pages and cover together.

4. Decorate the cover.

5. Make a page for each friend. You may want to put in pictures, phone numbers, birthdays, addresses, or other things you think would be fun.

TRY IT!

CITIZEN NEAR AND FAR

When you remember not to litter or when you collect used books for the library, you are being a good citizen. When you take soda cans to be recycled or collect cans of food for a food drive, you are being a good citizen. A citizen is a person who tries to help out wherever she is needed. These activities will help get you on your way!

Television and Newspaper Reporter

Learn about a story reported on television or the radio, or in a newspaper that showed how someone acted like a good citizen. Share your story with your troop or group. Pick one story and take turns being the "good citizen" and "the reporter."

More to Try: Create a skit or puppet play on good citizenship.

It's the Law

Children and adults have laws to obey. Rules and laws help make things fair for people.

You are meeting for the first time as Brownie Girl Scouts. You want to talk about all the fun things you hope to do this year. What special rules would you need to follow during the meeting? What rules would you need to follow when you go on trips? What might happen if you or your friends did not follow the rules?

Share your ideas with your troop. Look at the ideas again before your next meeting begins.

What Do You Think?

People are often asked to make choices. Sometimes people vote to tell others how they feel about certain choices.

Think of a time when your troop had to make choices. How did you make a decision?

Voting is one way to make a decision. Voting can be public, like raising your hand, or private, like marking a piece of paper and putting it in a box. Think of some decisions your troop needs to make. When would voting be a good way to choose? When would voting not be a good way to choose?

Calling All Helpers

At the United Nations, people get together from many different countries to talk about problems they share.

1. Think of a problem that affects people all over the world like recycling, homelessness, or acid rain.

2. Go home and talk to your parents and neighbors to find out how they think the problem should be solved.

3. At your next meeting, hold your "United Nations" meeting. Tell how people in your area of the community feel about the problem.

4. As a troop, think about everything that you heard and decide how best to handle the problem.

5. Share your solution with your family and neighbors.

Lead the Way

Think of a problem in your neighborhood. Look at the chart on pages 116–117. Plan your project using the questions from the chart. Do the project and share what you did with others.

Reach Out

As a citizen of the world, you can help other people in other countries with their problems. With the help of an adult, find a group in your community that works to help people in other countries. Try to visit this group or ask someone to come to a group/troop meeting to learn more about what they are doing to help people in other countries.

TRY IT!

COLORS AND SHAPES

3. Dip a sponge shape into one of the pans. Place it where you want on the paper and press. You can use this same shape over and over or you can add other shapes. Try other colors, too.

 rtists use colors, lines, and shapes to make art. How would you like to make your own? Try out your own creativity with these activities.

Stencil Stampers

You can make your own stamps to use over and over. Use these designs to create your own greeting cards or wrapping paper.

You will need:

- Old sponges
- Scissors
- Tempera paint
- Pans to hold the paint (old pie tins or baking pans are good)
- Paper to paint on
- Water (for cleanup)
- Construction paper
- Shelf paper

1. Cut the sponges into a shape you want.

2. Pour small amounts of paint into each pan.

More to Try: Try the Adinkra cloth activity on pages 91–92.

STENCIL STAMPER

Colors and Shapes Mobile

A mobile is a work of art that can move. Try making your own simple mobile.

You will need:

- Long plastic drinking straws
- Large needle
- Thick thread
- Cardboard
- Paints
- Crayons or markers

1. Thread the needle and tie a knot at the end of the thread. (Take care in using the needle. Be sure an adult or older person is around to help.)

2. Poke the needle through the straws to attach them. Use three, four, or five straws.

3. Tie a knot in the thread near the straws.

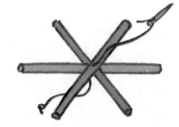

4. Cut the thread, leaving enough for you to hang the mobile.

5. Add colored shapes, which you can cut from the cardboard and paint, to your mobile by attaching them to the straws with a needle and thread. Hang them at different lengths.

6. Your mobile may tell a story or be on a subject that interests you. See the illustration for ideas.

7. Have someone help you balance your mobile.

Making Dough Shapes

You can mold and shape dough you make yourself.

You will need:

- 1 cup cornstarch
- 1 cup salt
- 1½ cups flour
- Water
- A mixing bowl
- A spoon

1. Put one cup of cornstarch, one cup of salt, and one and one-half cups of flour in the bowl.

2. Stir.

3. Add one-half cup of water and stir.

4. If the dough is still too stiff and dry, add one or two spoonfuls of water and mix with your hands.

5. You can make something with your dough after it is mixed, or you can save it for about two days in a plastic bag. Close the bag and keep it in a refrigerator until you are ready to use it.

6. Make something with your dough. Here are some ideas. Roll pieces of the dough into little balls of different sizes. Put the balls together to make things. Rub a little water on the balls to make them stick.

OR

Start with a ball the size of a lemon, and pull and pinch the clay to make a shape—an animal or a building, for example.

OR

Roll the dough into a ball that fits into your hand. Press your thumbs into the middle of the ball. Press the hole to make it bigger with one thumb while you turn the dough with the other hand. Keep doing this until the dough forms a pot or bowl shape.

Weaving Color Patterns

You will need:

- Sheets of different-colored paper
- Scissors
- Ruler
- Clear tape
- A pencil

1. Use the ruler to draw lines on the colored paper.

2. Make spaces between the lines the width of the ruler.

3. Cut the paper on the lines to make strips.

4. Lay eight or more strips of the same color next to each other evenly.

TRY IT•TRY IT•**TRY IT**•TRY IT•TRY IT•TRY IT•TRY IT•**TRY IT**•TRY IT•TRY IT•TRY IT•TRY IT•TRY IT•**TRY IT**•TRY IT

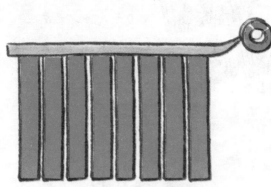

5. Tape them together very close to the top.

6. Take eight strips of another color.

7. One at a time, weave the strips in and out, as the picture shows.

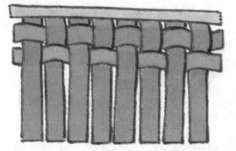

8. If you started on the top for the first row of weaving, start at the bottom for the next one. See the picture.

9. After you have woven all the strips, cut the extra edges and tape them together.

10. Turn your finished weaving over to see how it looks without the tape showing.

A Rainbow of Colors

You can mix your own colors. To learn how, try making your own painting. Start with only three colors. These three colors (red, blue, and yellow) are called "primary colors."

You will need:

- Poster paint or tempera in red, blue, and yellow
- Paper cups
- A paintbrush
- Paper
- A teaspoon

1. Mix your three primary colors to form other colors. Follow this guide when you are ready to mix a color.

red + blue = purple
blue + yellow = green
yellow + red = orange
red + blue + yellow = brown

2. Put two teaspoons of each of the colors you need in a cup and stir.

3. After you have mixed the colors, you are ready to paint.

4. Paint a picture.

More to Try: Use black and white paint to make more colors.

red + white = pink
blue + black = dark blue

Try some more combinations. What colors can you make?

Yarn paintings are a beautiful way to combine colors and shapes. Most yarn paintings are of animals or flowers.

You will need:

- Piece of cardboard
- Fine-tip pen
- Different colors of yarn or string
- Scissors
- White glue

1. Make an outline of your painting on the cardboard.

2. Cover the border with white glue.

3. Press a piece of yarn into the glue on the outline.

4. Fill in small areas with glue and then the yarn, using your fingers and scissors to press the yarn pieces tightly together. Always work from the outside in winding your yarn so it fills in all the spaces.

5. Let the glue dry and display your painting!

MEXICAN YARN PAINTING

TRY IT!

CREATIVE COMPOSING

Compose means "to put together," "to make up," "to create." Every person has creative abilities that she can use to compose something. You can learn about your own abilities by taking time to listen, to look, to hear, and to do. In this Try-It, you can have fun exploring creative composing.

Composing a Song

Read about Girl Scout ceremonies on pages 23–24 in the chapter "Welcome to Girls Scouts." Then compose or make up a song for a Girl Scout ceremony. Sing it alone or with your friends.

Composing a Poem

Compose a poem. Poems use words in special ways. Sometimes the words rhyme, which means they sound alike—scout and shout, sing and ring.

We must take care
And be sure to share,
Our world is our home.
(Can you think of any more
   lines?)

Sometimes the words create a design.

B-Z-Z-Z
Bees Buzzing all around...B-Z-Z-Z-Z

Sometimes each line has the same rhythm.

When **I** grow **up**,
I'll **be** a **Queen**,
And **never** have
To eat **stringbeans**.

When **I** ride **my** bike,
I move **so** quickly,
I **can't** see **the** world.

Follow these examples or try your own ideas. Share your poem with your family and friends.

Composing a Painting

Think of a special place. It can be a real place that you've seen or a make-believe place. Draw it lightly on a piece of paper in pencil. Look at where things are placed in your sketch. Should anything be moved? Should some things be made smaller? Should some be made larger? In a painting, the things that are closest to you are usually drawn bigger. Things that are farther away are usually smaller. Next, think of colors for your painting. You can use tempera, water-color, poster paints, felttip pens, chalk, crayons, or colored pencils. Hang your painting for others to see.

Composing a Message

Read about sign language on pages 77–78. Compose a sign message and sign it to someone.

Composing a Play

Make up a play about a person you admire or about one of the stories in this book. Work with friends or create a one-person play. Make invitations and perform your play.

Composing Music for Instruments

Compose a piece of music for an instrument. It can be an instrument you have made. Share the music with others.

DANCERCIZE

Physical exercise helps keep our bodies healthy. Some exercises can be done to music.

Aerobics

Exercise is a way to keep fit and have fun. Aerobic (air-row-bic) activity means you keep moving while your heart pumps harder. This makes your heart and lungs stronger.

You will need:

* A record or tape
* Record player or tape player
* Shorts and T-shirt or leotards and tights
* Sneakers

Note: Always do a warm-up activity before aerobic exercise. This one is from the Contemporary Issues book *Developing Health and Fitness: Be Your Best!*

Practice these movements to your favorite music.

* March in place.
* Step forward and backward and swing your arms to the sides.
* Step sideways and swing your arms in circles.
* Put your hands on your hips and move from side to side.
* Walk in a circle, lifting your knees very high while clapping your hands.

Make up some of your own moves. Do them for at least 10–15 minutes.

Always cool down after aerobic exercise. You can try some of these for your cool-down.

* Sit on the floor and make your legs into a "V." Reach over and try to touch your right toes. (Your knees can be slightly bent up.) Then try to reach your left toes. Be careful not to bounce.

- Keep your legs in a "V." Lean forward and stretch your arms out. Again, be careful not to bounce.
- Lie on your back. Bend your knees and bring them to your chest.

More to Try: Make up your own tape of music for exercising.

Dance on Stage

Watch a dance performance at a theater, outdoor stage, community center, or on television. What parts of the dance can you imitate? Describe this dance to others without using any words.

My Own Dance

Make up a dance to your favorite song or choose a song from this book and create a dance.

Dance Party

Have a dance party with a group of friends.

You will need:

- Records, tapes, or CDs
- A record player, tape player, or radio
- Snacks

1. Pick a time and place for a get-together with your friends.

2. Decide on the music. Each person can bring her favorite dance music.

3. Teach each other dance steps.

4. Have a healthy snack for energy.

Follow the Leader

Take turns with other girls in being the leader in your troop. The leader should call out a movement and show everyone how to follow it. You can do these movements to start: climbing a ladder, reaching for the sun on tiptoes, moving like a windmill, touching toes with knees slightly bent. Think of others you can do. Warm up for about five minutes.

Animal Moves

Play music while you make these animal moves. You can even match the music to the animal!

Rabbit jump: Bend your knees and jump forward.

Seal crawl: Pull yourself forward with your hands at your side while dragging your body and feet.

Elephant walk: Bend forward. Extend your arms and place one hand over the other, fingers pointed toward the ground, to form a trunk. Walk slowly with legs straight and trunk swinging from side to side.

Inchworm: Place both hands on the floor. Try to keep your knees stiff and legs straight, but bend your knees if you have to. Walk forward with your hands as far as you can, and then walk forward with your feet to your hands.

Crab walk: Sit on the floor with your hands behind you. Lift up your body with your hands and feet. Walk on all fours. Walk forward and backward in this position.

Frog jump: Squat on the floor with hands in front of feet. Jump forward and land on both hands and feet.

Make up your own animal moves and try them.

Seal Crawl

Frog Jump

Inchworm

Crab Walk

Elephant Walk

Rabbit Jump

EARTH AND SKY

ook down. Look up. What do you see? Earth below and sky above!

The Soil

Find a special spot in an outdoor area.

You will need:

- A magnifying glass
- A spoon or small trowel
- A pencil or tweezers
- White paper or a plastic dish
- A yard of string

1. Make a circle on the ground with your string. Look on the surface inside your circle. What do you find? Do you find plants? What about animals? Is there anything else?

2. Next, dig three small holes in your circle so that you can look below the surface of the top layer of soil or forest litter. Can you find differences in plants and animals as you dig down one inch, three inches, and six inches? Is there a difference in how the soil feels or in its color as you go deeper? Use your white paper or plastic dish to help you study soil critters as you find them.

3. Share your findings with someone or the group. Carefully fill the holes and leave your circle as you found it.

Going, Going, Gone

On a walk or hike, examine the edge of a stream or a place where the ground is bare on a hillside or slope. Look for places where soil has been worn down or disappeared.

Find out what causes soil erosion. In the backyard or in a sandbox, build a mound of soil about two feet high or knee-high. Pretend that this is a hill or mountainside in your community. Wet the hill with a watering can or a slow, steady stream of water from a hose. What happens to your hill? Find a slope that is covered with grass or plants. Water it with your watering can. What happens? Is the result different from what happens on your mountain of soil?

The Sky's My Home!

Find a place outside where you can sit and be a "sky watcher." Observe the types of creatures in the air. Also observe the ways these creatures move. Share what you observe with others by acting out the movements.

More to Try: Build a feeder for a creature of the sky. Be alert for what comes to visit your feeder.

Our Air

Can you see the air? Be an air quality inspector.

You will need:

- A roll of tape
- Some string about 2 feet long

1. Find a spot out-of-doors protected from rain and strong winds where you can tie your string. Tie it about chest-high. You can use thumbtacks to tack down the ends.

2. Each day for three weeks, take a strip of tape about three inches long and write the date on the non-stick side. Put a piece of tape on the string so that the sticky side is on the outside. At the end of three weeks, you should have a record of particles from the air. Which tape strip is the cleanest? On what day did you notice a change? What do you think is in the particles in the air that you can see?

Rooting Around

Trees and most plants send roots into the ground to take in water and minerals. Plants have different kinds of roots. Some roots go deep for water way underground. Some spread wide to catch rainwater as it falls. Start a plant and see some roots grow.

① Carrot

② Avocado

Hot and Cold

Learn how to use a thermometer safely. What temperature makes water freeze? What point makes it boil? What is your normal body temperature? Try the activities about the sun on page 138 in "How and Why."

1. Cut the top of a carrot. Push four toothpicks on the sides. Rest on top of a jar or glass filled with water.

2. Do the same thing with an avocado seed.

3. Take a stem with leaves from a plant. Put it into water.

③ Stem with leaves

EARTH IS OUR HOME

Y ou, all other people, and plants and animals share the earth. How can you make your home a better place?

How Long Does It Take?

Collect a sample of trash and garbage to create your own landfill. Include plastic, glass, aluminum, fast-food containers, soda straws, plant clippings, grass, an apple core, some orange rind, a stick of gum, a candy wrapper, and some newspaper.

1. Put the trash into an old nylon stocking. Make a list and a drawing of what goes into the stocking as a record.

2. Bury the stocking completely in the earth and mark the location. Don't bury it near water because it might make the water polluted.

3. Wait two or three months. Dig up the stocking and the trash. What do you discover? Be sure to wear gloves and avoid touching items in your landfill. You might use a stick or a small trowel to look at the items in your stocking. Have any of the items changed? How have

they changed? Are there some things in your stocking that will keep a lifetime? What happens to garbage that leaves your house? Does it get buried like your stocking? Is any of it recycled? Does it get hauled to a dump far away from your town?

More to Try: Keep track of how many bags of trash your family throws out each day, week, or month.

Recycling

Read about recycling on pages 145–147. Then recycle something.

Trash Busters

Participate in a community cleanup day or adopt a special place for the troop year. Care for your place and let others know about your efforts. Remember to wear clothing and gloves that protect you if you help clean up.

Oil Spill

Try the "Oil Spill" activity on page 145.

SOLAR COOKER

You can use the sun's energy to cook your food in the outdoors. Follow the chart at right to build a solar oven. You will need to ask an adult to help you measure and cut. Building hints: Appliance boxes make good ovens. Place the shiny side of the foil so that it faces out when glueing onto cardboard. Foil should not be on the outside of your oven because you want the box to soak up the sun's heat. Foil is on the inside of the box to bounce heat onto the black cooking pans.

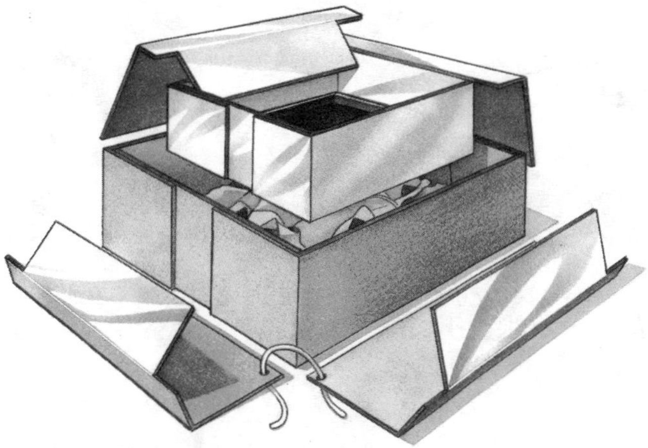

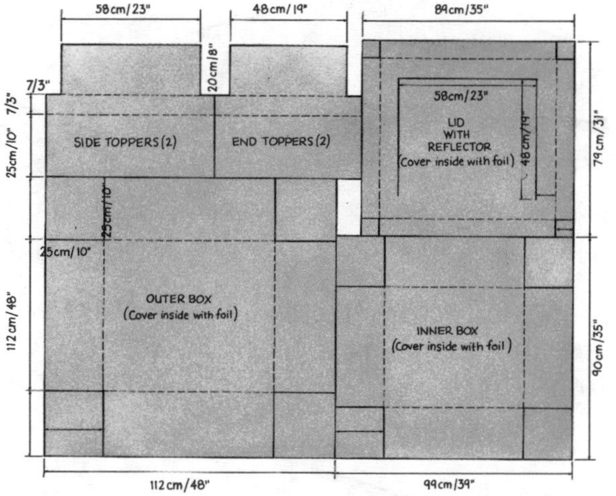

HERE'S WHAT YOU WILL NEED:
Single plate of glass; corrugated cardboard for two large boxes with one lid and four "toppers"; aluminum foil; glue; insulation (crumpled newspaper); a dark metal tray; string; and a stick or wire.

The chart diagram:

58cm/23"	48cm/19"	89cm/35"
SIDE TOPPERS (2)	END TOPPERS (2)	LID WITH REFLECTOR (Cover inside with foil) 58cm/23" 48cm/19"
OUTER BOX (Cover inside with foil) 25cm/10"		INNER BOX (Cover inside with foil)

7/3" 20cm/8" 25cm/10" 7/3" 23cm/10" 25cm/10" 112cm/48" 112cm/48" 99cm/39" 79cm/31" 40cm/35"

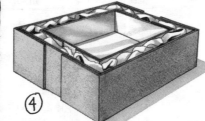

① Glue aluminum foil to both sides of the inner box and to one side of the lid and the upper halves of the end and side toppers. (Outer box should be uncovered.)

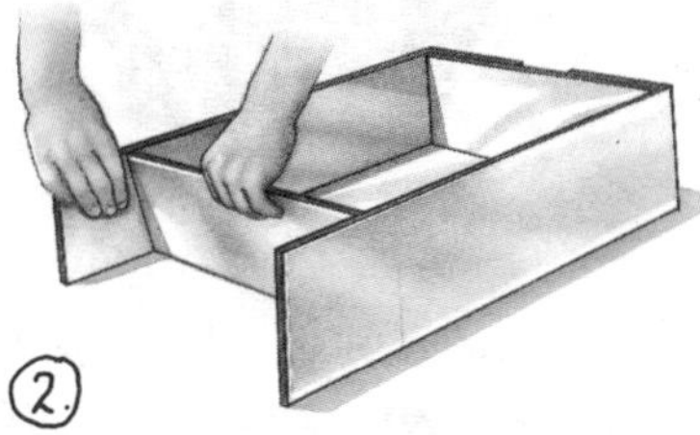

② Score and fold the inner and outer boxes.

③ Fill the bottom of the outer box with 2 inches of insulation to support inner box.

④ Add the inner box and fill the sides with more insulation.

⑤ Fold and place toppers over the edges of the boxes.

⑥ Put the black tray in the bottom of the inner box. Tie or glue the outer flaps.

⑦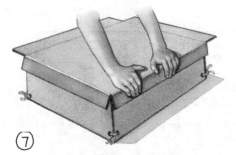

Score and fold reflector lid over the finished box. Glue the corners.

⑧

Make three measured cuts inside the lid to make the reflector flap.

⑨

Spread glue or caulk around edge of glass.

⑩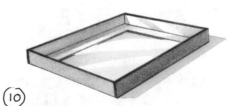

Press glass to inside of lid until glue is dry.

⑪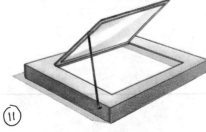

Fold up flap and attach a stick or wire to adjust the height.

⑫

Put food into <u>black</u> pot and cover with a <u>black</u> lid. (Shiny pots cook poorly.)

⑬

Place the pot in the center of the cooker and replace the reflector lid.

⑭

Face your cooker toward the sun. Adjust the flap so that light reflects onto the pot. Leave closed until cooked (See chart). No need to stir, food will not burn. Rotate box if necessary to capture sunlight.

TYPE OF FOOD AND COOKING TIME ON A SUNNY DAY

For 10 pounds (4 kilos) of food

<u>Easy to cook (1-2 hours)</u>	<u>Medium (3-4 hours)</u>	<u>Hard to cook (5 hours)</u>
Eggs	Potatoes	Most dried beans
Rice	Pastry	Large roast (all meats get more tender)
Fish	Some beans, lentils	
Chicken	Most meats	
Fruit	Bread	
Vegetables (above ground)	Vegetables (roots)	

TO PASTEURIZE WATER:
Small jar : 2 hours
Large jar : 4 hours

COOKING TIME IS LONGER:
- With larger amounts of food
- If partly cloudy
- When the sun is lower in the sky

Sun Pretzels

2 1/4 cups baking mix   2 tablespoons vegetable oil
2/3 cup lowfat milk   1 egg   salt

Combine baking mix, milk and oil. Stir 20 times.
Form dough gently into a ball. Knead 5 times. Form
dough into 32 strips the size of a pencil. Bend into
pretzel shape. Beat egg. Brush pretzels with egg
and sprinkle them with salt. Bake in solar
oven on dark baking sheet for 20-30 minutes or
until done.

Recipe for a Miniworld

A terrarium is a small world in an enclosure and is made up of living things, soil, water, and air. It is surrounded by a covering that lets in light. The earth we live on is covered by air and is like a huge terrarium. Plants and animals need soil, air, water, and light in order to survive in both a terrarium and on the earth. If any of these things are missing or are damaged by pollution, the plants and animals will suffer.

Have someone help you make your own healthy terrarium. Here are some things to use:

- A clear wide-mouthed jar (like a peanut butter jar)
- 2 handfuls of small rocks or sand
- 2 handfuls of soil
- 1 handful of dead leaves
- Some moss from a forest, a vacant lot, or elsewhere
- Several small ferns or plants from a forest, a vacant lot, or a plant store

(Do not pick protected plants or overpick an area. Ask permission to gather materials if you are not on your own property.)

Follow these steps to make your terrarium.

1. Put the sand in first, then the soil, and layer them evenly. Place the dead leaves on top.

2. Using a pencil, tongs, or a chopstick, make holes. Then plant your plants. Use the moss to fill in around the plants after you have tapped the soil down gently.

3. Water your world with a squeeze bottle or sprinkle water with your hands, but do not drench your world.

4. Place the lid on your jar. Keep the lid closed, as your world should have everything it needs to survive. Place the jar in good light, but not directly in the sunlight.

Observe your terrarium daily. You might want to keep a diary of what you see or make some sketches. Watch for changes. Are there any new plants or animals? How do you think they got there? What do you think would happen if you removed your terrarium from light? What do you think would happen if you put it in direct sunlight?

FOOD FUN

OR

Bake in 375° F. oven for 40–45 minutes. Put marshmallow on top of each apple for last 2–5 minutes, until melted.

5. Apples should be tender, but not mushy.

6. Enjoy hot or cold!

Recipe Fun

Try this activity from *Developing Health and Fitness: Be Your Best!*, the Contemporary Issues booklet. Collect recipes from different cultures that include grains and starches, like rice, noodles, quinoa, kasha, polenta, cous-cous, and many others. Try some in your troop or group.

Snacks for Girl Scouts

Here are two snacks to try at Girl Scout get-togethers.

1. Vegetable snacks. Make the "walking salad" on page 156 in the chapter "How and Why?"

Eating the right foods is very important for your health.

Baked Apples

You will need:
- 1 tart baking apple for each person
- 1/4 cup unsweetened apple juice for each apple
- 2 tablespoonfuls of raisins for each apple
- 1 marshmallow for each apple
- Some ground cinnamon

1. Have an adult help you peel the apples halfway down. Core the apples almost to their bottoms.

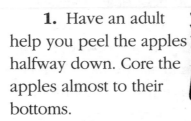

2. Stuff the core with raisins.

3. Put apples in baking or microwave pan. Pour juice over apples. Sprinkle each with cinnamon.

4. Bake in microwave on high for 8–10 minutes. Melt marshmallow on each apple for last minute/30 seconds.

2. Fruit juice fizz.
You will need:

- 1 orange or lemon
- Orange juice
- Pineapple juice
- Cranberry juice
- Seltzer or club soda
- A bowl
  or pitcher
- A knife

1. Cut the orange or lemon into slices.

2. Put one or two cups of each juice into the pitcher.

3. Add three more cups of juice for every cup of seltzer or club soda.

4. Chill the juice.
5. Serve.

Sloppy Joes

Here is a fun recipe you can make with your Girl Scout friends or your family. It is especially good when you make it outdoors! The Girl Guides of Canada submitted it to *World Games and Recipes*. The recipe will serve 4–6 people.

You will need:

- 1 pound of ground beef or chicken
- 1 can of tomato or chicken soup, or half of each
- Ketchup
- Prepared mustard
- Hamburger buns or French bread
- Skillet
- Container to hold excess fat
- Strainer
- Stove top, hot plate, or outdoor oven

1. Brown the meat in the skillet.

2. Hold the strainer over the container for fat. Pour everything in the skillet into the strainer. It will catch the meat and let the fat run through. You can also rinse the meat in the strainer under hot water to get off more fat.

3. Put the meat back in the skillet. Add the soup, ketchup, and mustard. Heat until thoroughly cooked.

4. Serve on the buns or French bread. Yum!

Food for a Day

Make your own breakfast, lunch, and dinner for a day. Use your favorite recipes. Ask an adult to help you plan.

Food Pyramid

Read about the food pyramid on page 39 in "Taking Care of Yourself and Your Home" and try the activities on these pages.

TRY IT!
GIRL SCOUT WAYS

Being a Girl Scout makes you part of a very special group of people! Here are some activities that show some of the things Girl Scouts everywhere know.

About Girl Scouting

In the chapter "Welcome to Girl Scouts" you learned about many of the things that make Girl Scouting special. This activity is about some of those things you learned.

Reread the section on "The Girl Scout Promise and Law" in the chapter "Welcome to Girl Scouts." Try the activities in that section.

OR

Make up a puppet show or play that tells about the Girl Scout Law. Show it to some new Girl Scouts or to girls who want to become Girl Scouts.

Special Girl Scout Ways

Reread the section about "Special Girl Scout Ways." Practice the hand signs listed below and show them to someone who is new to Girl Scouting.

- Girl Scout handshake
- Girl Scout sign
- Quiet sign
- Friendship circle
- Friendship squeeze
- Girl Scout sayings

Ceremonies

Ceremonies are a very special part of Girl Scouting. You can learn about them and practice doing them with this activity. Be sure to read pages 23–24 to find out all about ceremonies. Plan a ceremony for one of Girl Scouting's special days.

Girl Scout Birthday

Juliette Low started the first Girl Scout troop on March 12, 1912. This day is the Girl Scout birthday. Plan a party for this day. See page 25 for more ideas on ways to celebrate.

S'mores

This is a special sweet treat that is not an everyday snack. You'll probably want to try it on a camping trip or at a cookout. Find out why it's called "S'mores."

You will need:

- Graham crackers
- Large marshmallows
- Milk chocolate bars
- A long stick or roasting wire to hold over the fire

1. Break the graham crackers into a square shape (see the picture).

2. Break the chocolate bar into a square the same size as the cracker or smaller. Put this square on top of the graham cracker (see the picture).

3. Put one or two marsh-mallows on the end of the stick.

4. Use the stick to hold the marshmallows over the fire, but not too close (see the picture).

5. When the marshmallows start to melt just a little, take them off the stick and put them on top of the chocolate bar square (see the picture).

6. Put another graham cracker square on top of the marshmallows.

7. Eat it! Now do you know why they're called S'mores?

(Be careful that your marshmallow and/or stick do not catch on fire. If they do, do not wave them around. Carefully blow them out or let them burn. Always be careful with your stick and never play near or in the fire.)

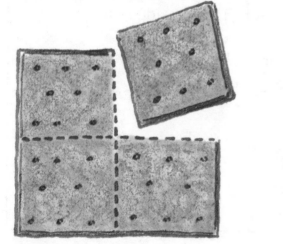

~ Sit~Upon ~

Girl Scouts make sit-upons to use when the ground is damp or too hot or cold and they want to keep their clothes clean. You can make your own to use at troop meetings, camping events, or other Girl Scout get-togethers. Follow these steps and look at the pictures for help.

You will need:

- A large piece of waterproof material (like an old plastic tablecloth or shower curtain or a plastic garbage bag)
- Newspapers or other stuffing
- A yarn needle
- Yarn or string

1. Cut the waterproof material into two large squares big enough for you to sit on.

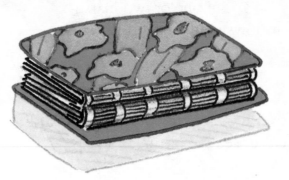

2. Put newspapers or old rags between the two squares to form a cushion.

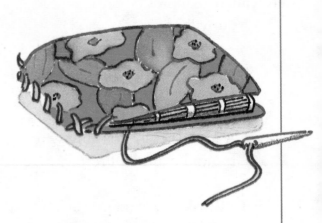

3. Sew the two squares together with yarn or string, using the yarn needle. Have an adult show you how to use the needle safely. Be sure to sew completely around the edges of the sit-upon.

TRY IT!

GOOD FOOD

In "Taking Care of Yourself and Your Home," you read about good nutrition. Here are some good food activities.

Smart Shopper

Labels list the ingredients in a food product, starting with the largest amount down to the smallest amounts. Cut out or remove lists of ingredients from cereal cartons, cake-mix boxes, and canned and frozen foods. Check the labels to see if sugar or salt is in the list of ingredients. Many times, sugar or salt is added to food as a flavoring. Too much sugar or salt is not good for you. Sugar is sometimes called corn syrup, sucrose, glucose, or fructose. Salt may be listed as sodium. Find three labels that have little or no salt. Try to eat these or other foods with little or no salt.

Great Groceries

Help your family make up a grocery list. Write down foods your family likes to eat during the week. Look at the list with the person who does the food shopping in your home. Go with her or him to the grocery store to help choose good foods. Then plan at least one meal using what you have learned from the food pyramid.

Dairy Foods

1. Many kinds of foods come from milk, such as yogurt, butter, and ice cream. Bring several kinds of these foods to your meeting for a taste test. Which one is your favorite?

2. Try making some new flavors of yogurt. Get some plain, low-fat or no-fat yogurt. Then, set out small bowls of different toppings: crunchy cereal, strawberries, bananas, peanut butter, blueberries, apple slices, nuts, honey, and other fruits. Have fun eating your unique dessert.

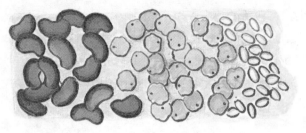

Proteins

Protein helps your body while you are growing. Beans are an inexpensive and healthy way to get protein. Find out about beans!

1. Bring in samples of dry beans.

2. Find three recipes for cooked dry beans.

3. In your troop meeting, or with an adult at home, make a bean recipe. Try to mix two or three kinds of beans with some vegetables, sauce, or salad dressing.

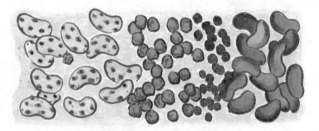

Plenty of Pasta

You learned from the food pyramid that you need to eat a lot of food from the bread, cereal, rice, or pasta group every day. Pasta (like spaghetti or other noodles) is easy and quick to cook and tastes good too. It comes in many shapes and sizes and colors. Find out about pasta that is made from spinach, whole wheat, or other foods.

You and your Brownie Girl Scout friends can make your own healthy and colorful pasta.

You will need:

- All kinds of pasta, in different shapes and colors
- A large pot for boiling water
- Colander or strainer
- Individual plates
- Forks
- Stove
- Two kinds of sauce (see at right)

Sauce One

- 1 small onion chopped
- Package of frozen broccoli
- Package of frozen carrots (pieces)
- Package of frozen chopped zucchini or yellow squash
- Package of frozen peas
- 1 can low-salt chicken broth (or make with chicken boullion cubes)
- 1 tablespoon olive oil

Thaw vegetables. In large frying pan, heat olive oil. Carefully cook onion until yellow and soft. Add broth and vegetables. Cook until firm. Serve over pasta.

Sauce Two

- 1 can of puréed tomatoes
- Dried oregano
- Dried basil
- 1 bunch parsley
- Grated Parmesan or Romano cheese

Heat tomatoes in pan, stirring them slowly. Break off bits of parsley and add to tomatoes. Add dried spices to taste. Add two tablespoons grated cheese to sauce. Heat until almost bubbling. Pour over pasta and serve. Add more cheese if you like.

Cooking Pasta

1. Fill the pot with water until it is almost full. Put it on the stove to boil.

2. When the water is boiling, add the pasta.

3. Put the lid on the pot and turn down the temperature on the stove.

4. After about ten minutes, the pasta should be done. With an adult, carefully take the pot to the sink. Pour everything into the colander.

5. Serve a little bit of pasta on each girl's plate.

6. Add sauce and cheese; serve.

Brownie Soup

You can make Brownie Soup. This recipe should get bigger with each girl who adds to it. Use what you learned in the "Smart Shopper" activity to help you choose the ingredients. Remember, an adult must be with you to be sure you're safe when cooking.

You will need:

- A can opener
- A large spoon
- A large pot
- Bowls
- Spoons
- Ladle
- 4 cups of broth (low-sodium is best)
- 3 cups of different kinds of vegetables
- 1 cup of beans
- ½ cup of rice or ½ cup of small noodles (*Everybody should help decide on an ingredient*).

1. Put the vegetables and one cup of water into the pot. Stir.

2. Heat until hot.

3. Serve.

4. Clean up.

TRY IT!

HER STORY

An issue is a subject or topic that people may have strong feelings about and want to discuss. How can you learn about issues important to women and children?

A Girl Scout's Story

Read the Juliette Gordon Low story on pages 8–12 in the chapter "Welcome to Girl Scouts." Then try to find a woman in your community who has been a member of Girl Scouting for a long time. Invite her to speak to your troop, if possible. Think of some questions you can ask her. Find out about her memories of being a Girl Scout.

Talk to Women

This activity is a requirement. Ask at least three women of different ages (from teenagers to women over 55 years old) what are the five most important issues facing women today. Include at least two women from a race or ethnic group different from your own. Tell others what you learned from the women.

More to Try: Make a chart to show what you found. Which issue was named most often? What does this tell you about the important issues in your community?

Create Tales

What are some of your favorite fables and fairy tales? Would these stories be different if they were written today? How would the women in the story be different? be the same? Modernize some stories. How can you share your "modern" stories with others?

A CEREMONY TO HONOR WOMEN

Plan a simple ceremony to honor women. You can recite poems written by girls or women or perform a skit or make up a song about a woman in history or in your community. If you can play an instrument, play along to the song. Invite women who are special to you to attend the ceremony.

Help in Your Community

Read the story starting on page 111 in the chapter "Leadership in Girl Scouting and Beyond." What did the girls find out? Service is an important part of being a Girl Scout. Look at the section on service that follows the story. Choose a service project you would like to do, and follow the action steps given.

Your Story

Think about where you will be when you are a grownup. Create a time line like the one on page 38, but write in what you would like to do or to have happen in your future.

TRY IT!
HOBBIES

	YES	NO
Is this hobby fun?	___	___
Will this hobby be too expensive?	___	___
Do I have enough room in my home to do this hobby?	___	___
Will this hobby hurt the environment?	___	___
Is this hobby safe?	___	___
Do I have enough time for this hobby?	___	___

A hobby is something that you like to do when you have some free time. Hobbies can be collecting things, like shells or rocks, making things, like knitting or drawing, or doing things, like reading or playing a sport.

Your Talents, Interests, and Hobbies

Most people start a hobby because they are interested in something or because they are good at doing something. On pages 66–67, you listed your interests and talents.

What hobby ideas can you get from your lists?

New Ideas

You are exploring many new things in Brownie Girl Scouts. Look through this book. What activities do you like the most? Make a list. Would these make good hobbies?

Getting Started

Before starting any hobby, you should ask yourself these questions. Then, talk about starting a hobby with your family.

How can you find out the right answers to these questions? Whom should you ask?

Types of Hobbies

What are some things you can collect? Make a list here.

_____

_____

_____

Maybe you have already begun a collection and don't even know it! Look around your home. Do you already have two or three or more things that can make a collection?

What are some hobbies that you can do? Make a list here.

_____

_____

_____

What are some hobbies that you can make? Make a list here.

_____

_____

_____

Organizing Your Hobby

If you are starting a collection, try organizing it. When you organize a collection, you give each thing a label with its special name and write other special information on the label. You also make an arrangement of your collection. Your collection should be easy and attractive to see. What ideas can you get to arrange your own collection?

Practicing Your Hobby

Hobbies, like sports, need practice. Make some time every week to practice your hobby. Here's a chart. Fill in the time you spend on your hobby. Once you have practiced your hobby, try teaching it to others.

Monday _____

Tuesday _____

Wednesday _____

Thursday _____

Friday _____

Saturday _____

Sunday _____

Try doing your hobby with some other people who practice your hobby.

Making an Example

If your hobby is making things, like knitting, drawing, or making models, make an example. Show some other people how you make it.

Make a way of displaying your hobby. Make a label that describes the work you did.

Find someone who has the same hobby. What more about your hobby can you learn from this person?

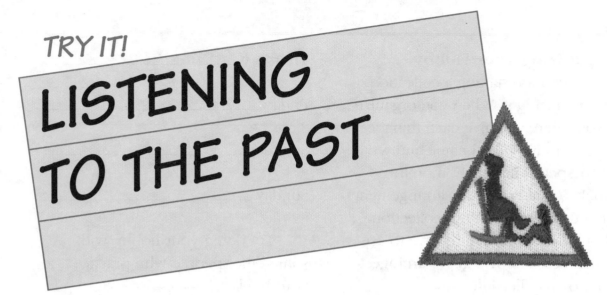

LISTENING TO THE PAST

Everybody has a story to tell, a story about her family, her special interests, and her life in general. When you listen to someone talk about his or her life, you are participating in oral history.

Listen to the Stories

Read pages 74–75 about family history and try the activities.

Community Stories

Get to know the stories of some of the oldest people in your community. You might get someone in your family to introduce you. Or, contact a senior citizens' group for help. Find some way to share these stories with the community.

Know Your Town

Visit an old cemetery in your area. Do the following activities.

1. Look for the oldest dates on the tombstones you see. Write them down. How old were these people when they died?

2. Write down the most unusual names.

3. Take pictures of the most unusual tombstones.

4. Find out the most common name there.

Become a Storyteller

Choose three stories written in the past or about the past and tell them to others.

OR

Act out the three stories you choose.

Games of Yesteryear

Hopscotch, paddleball, jacks, and stickball are some favorite games from long ago. Try playing jacks. You can use ten small shells, pebbles, or beans if you can't find jacks. You also need a small ball that fits in the palm of your hand. Bounce the ball, try to pick up as many jacks as you can, and catch the ball before it bounces again. You can try picking up one jack, then two, then three without touching any others. You can try picking up jacks with the jacks you've already picked up still in your hand. How else can you play jacks?

Community Record

Try the activity "Explore Your Neighborhood," on page 85.

MANNERS

When you meet new people or when you're with your family and friends, good manners show that you are considerate.

Table Manners

Pretend you are at a restaurant. Take turns being the server and the customer. Talk about polite and impolite ways to act in a restaurant. You can have even more fun by using sample menus from restaurants in the community and a place setting (plates, cups, silverware) for each person.

More to Try: Many cultures use tableware different from a knife and fork and spoon. You could use chopsticks, a special spoon, or just your right hand. You might also have different table settings or one large bowl for the family. Learn about some other ways to eat.

Happy Helper

Good manners can mean helping at home. Think of a job you could do that an adult does now. Offer to do the job for one week. Could you keep doing this job?

Respect for Others

Showing respect for others means treating them the way you want to be treated. The Girl Scout Law states, "I will do my best to show respect for myself and others through my words and actions."

Repeat the Girl Scout Law. Think of as many ways as you can to show respect for others. Talk about things you can do when people are not respectful to you and others. Create a song, skit, or group poem.

Phone Fun

Practice the right way to use the telephone. In pairs, act out some conversations.

1. Someone in the house needs help.

2. Someone from your mother's workplace wants to leave a message.

3. Your grandmother calls you to chat.

Meeting People

Good manners include knowing how to introduce yourself and others. Introductions are different in different cultures. Meeting someone new may be the first step in making a new friend.

Try the following activity on introductions at home and away from home.

1. Practice introducing yourself to others in your troop, at home, and in school. Include a smile, a handshake, and a friendly hello. Say something like "Hi, my name is. . . ."

2. Practice introducing other people. Introductions are made in a certain order. The common rule is that you say a woman's or older person's name first, as well as the name of people with important positions or titles. For example, you would say, "Ms. Lewis, I'd like you to meet Alexis Smith. Alexis, this is Ms. Lewis." The following list contains ideas for practicing introductions:

- A new girl in your troop
- A friend to a parent
- A girl to a boy
- A person with a special title or degree, such as father, rabbi, doctor, or judge. Try using a person's job title—for example, "Hello, Dr. Jones, I am. . . ."

Practice these greetings used in different parts of the world:

- In Japan, a bow is a traditional greeting.
- In Chile, a handshake and a kiss to the right cheek are customary.
- In Fiji, a smile and an upward movement of the eyebrows are how people greet one another.

More to Try: Learn titles that are used in other languages and cultures. For example, "Señora" is the Spanish title for a married woman. In Japan, "San" is used after someone's name to show respect for the person. In Turkey, an older woman calls a younger woman "Canim," which means "dear" or "beloved." In this country, Navajo people use the term "Hosteen," which means uncle, for older men they admire. Can you find some others?

Parties

Pretend you are a party host. What should a host do so that her guests have a good time? Pretend you are a party guest. How is a good guest considerate?

MATH FUN

Did you know that you use math every day? When you count money, or measure your height and weight, or tell time, you are using math.

My Numbers

Numbers are used to tell many things about you. For instance, you use numbers to tell how old you are. Think of the many things about yourself that can be described with numbers. How many toes do you have? Make a "My Numbers" poster that tells all your important numbers facts.

Can You Guess?

Find out how well your friends and family can guess amounts. Find a large jar with a lid. Fill it with something like seeds, beans, or marbles. Count each one as you fill the jar. Have at least five people guess the number of objects that are in the jar. Ask family and friends to record their guesses and how they made them. Let them pick up the jar if they wish. Did anyone make a close guess?

Math and Me

Read page 38 and do the time line activity about yourself. Share it with other girls in your troop or group. How are you alike? How are you different?

Measure Up

Read page 129 in the "How and Why?" chapter. Try the stick of gum measuring activities.

Working Together

Read about planning a budget on page 121. Think of three activities your troop would like to do and plan a budget for each one.

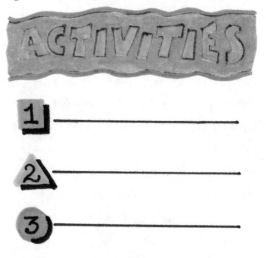

ACTIVITIES

1 _____

2 _____

3 _____

Alphabet Code

Make up your own secret code. Write down the letters of the alphabet. Next to each letter put a different number from 1 to 26. You don't have to write the numbers in order.

Use your code to send a secret message.

More to Try: Give a dollar value to each letter of the alphabet. For example, A = $1.00, B = $2.00, C = $3.00, and so on. Then add up the dollars that are in the letters of your first name. You may use pencil and paper or a calculator if you have one. Find the most expensive word or name you can.

TRY IT!

ME AND MY SHADOW

A shadow is formed when a body or object blocks light. Artists study how light falls on things to create shadows, and use this knowledge in their paintings, photographs, and other artwork.

Making Shadow Bags

You will need:

- A paper shopping bag with handles
- Scissors
- Tape or glue
- Colored construction paper
- Colored cellophane paper

Cut out designs on the sides of your shopping bag. Tape the colored paper and the colored cellophane paper from the inside over parts of your design. Leave some parts of the design open so light can come through. Use the bag to carry things, as a decoration, or give it to someone as a gift.

Tracing Your Shadow

With a partner, stand so your shadow falls on a big piece of paper taped to a wall or the floor. Stand still while your partner traces your shadow. Then do the same for your partner. Try creating some different shadow shapes.

Making Shadow-and-Light Plaques

Read about tools in the section "Home Repairs" in the chapter "Taking Care of Yourself and Your Home." Collect some lightweight aluminum pans (like the ones frozen pies come in). With a felt marker, draw a design on a pan. Place the pan on a table or counter. Put lots of newspaper between the pan and the table so you don't damage the surface. Punch holes in the aluminum with a hammer and nails of different sizes. Place your pan plaque against a window or lamp so that light can pass through the nail holes and highlight your design.

218 TRY IT•TRY IT•TRY IT•TRY IT•TRY IT•TRY IT•TRY IT•TRY IT•TRY IT•TRY IT•TRY IT•TRY IT•TRY IT•TRY IT•TRY IT•TRY IT

Keeping Shadows

Take some pictures of interesting shadows that you see outdoors. You may need an adult to help you. You can use black-and-white film. Notice how things look in light, in shade, and in the dark. Make a display of your photos of interesting shadows.

OR

You will need some light-sensitive paper from an art supply store or clean fresh newspaper or newsprint. Place an object on the shiny side of the paper or on the newspaper in bright sunlight. After a few minutes for the paper or a half-hour for the newspaper, you should be able to see a shadow image.

Shadow Box

Tell a favorite story in a shadow box. Get a shoe box or other small box, paper and cardboard, glue, tape, scissors, and scraps of wood, ribbon, fabric, and other materials. Decorate the inside of your box to tell a scene from your story.

DOING A SHADOW PLAY

Make a shadow theater with a bright light bulb and some white sheets. Choose a play with lots of action and invite an audience to your performance.

MOVERS

3. Then go around to the other three corners and fold them the same way.

How many ways do things move? These activities will help you find out.

1. Cut paper squares, following the dotted lines on the diagram.

4. Poke the pin through the middle of the paper and then into the end of the straw or stick.

Wind Wheels

Try this experiment to see how moving air has energy to move things.

You will need:

- Square sheets of stiff paper
- Straight pins
- Straws or thin wooden sticks, 8″ or more long

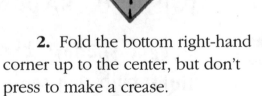

2. Fold the bottom right-hand corner up to the center, but don't press to make a crease.

5. If the point comes through the straw or stick, cover the point with clay, glue, or other material. Or bend the end down and cover with tape.

You can decorate the paper before making the wind wheel. Find out the different ways you can make the machine spin. Hold it over a lighted bulb. Blow on it. Run with it. What happens? Your wind wheel is a pinwheel.

Find out about windmills—where they are, what they are used for, and how they work.

Energy Saver

In the chapter "How and Why?" you read about ways to save energy. Did you know some machines can store energy, too? Try this simple experiment to find out that something can move and save energy at the same time.

You will need:

- A coffee can
- 2 plastic coffee can lids
- 2 rubber bands
- String
- Nuts or bolts

1. With an adult, cut off the ends of the coffee can so that you have a cylinder (sil-un-der).

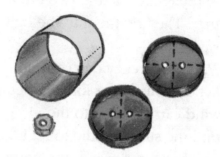

2. Punch two holes about two inches apart, on each lid. Make sure they are an equal distance from the center of the lid.

3. Cut open each rubber band. Thread each one through the holes of the lids, and retie the ends.

4. Join the two rubber bands inside the coffee can by tying them together with a piece of string. Tie a weight, such as a nut or bolt, onto the string.

5. Snap the lids onto the can. Try to roll the can across the floor. What happens?

Wind, Clouds, and Rain

Read about "Wind" and "Clouds and Rain" on pages 138–140 in the chapter "How and Why?" and try one of the activities on those pages.

Go Fly a Kite

When a kite is held into the wind, air pushes the kite upward so it can fly. Make your own kite.

You will need:

- Thin paper (like newspaper), 3 feet by 2½ feet
- Thin sticks (like bamboo, cane, or balsa)
- A ball of string
- Tape
- Glue
- Scissors

1. Pick two sticks for the frame. One stick must be twice as long as the other one.

2. Cross the sticks and tie them with the string. Run string around the edges to make a diamond shape.

3. Lay the frame on the paper. Cut around the frame so that you have about one and one-half inches all around.

4. Fold the paper over the frame and glue it down. Let it dry.

5. Make a tail for your kite with a piece of string about twice as long as the kite. Tie the tail onto the kite.

6. Tie two short strings to the long stick of the frame, above and below the cross. Tie the two ends together. Then tie them to the ball of string.

7. On a breezy day (but not too windy), take your kite and let the wind carry it up into the air. Unwind the string a little to let it go higher. You can run into the wind to get off to a good start.

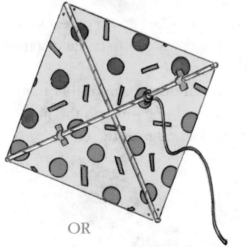

OR

Read pages 92–93 about kite-flying in Thailand. Try making a kite.

Fliers

Try making these paper fliers. The air holds them up and their shape makes them fly in different patterns.

You will need:

- Sheets of paper the size of this book (construction paper or magazine covers work well)
- Scissors
- A drinking straw
- Tape
- Paper clips

Helicopter

1. Cut the paper in half the long way. You'll only need one of those halves.

2. Fold the paper in half the long way, then fold in half the long way again.

3. Fold the paper in the middle.

4. Fold the ends, as the diagram shows.

5. Weight the bottom with a paper clip.

6. Drop your helicopter from a high point to see it fly.

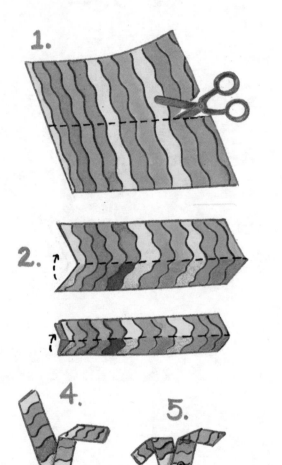

Circle Glider

1. Fold a piece of paper in half the long way. Fold it in half the long way again.

2. Make two strips by cutting along the folds. Give a friend the other strips for her glider.

3. Cut the width of one of your strips in half.

4. Make a loop with the long strip, and paper clip it to the straw. Put the small loop of the clip into the straw.

5. Loop the half-strip and paper clip it to the other end of the straw.

6. With the short loop facing forward, give your glider a quick toss to send it flying.

Twig Rafts

These small rafts are like the bigger ones that used to cross rivers and streams years ago. You can sail them in the bathtub or pool or on a waterway.

You will need:

- 14 straight twigs, or sticks 10″ long
- String
- White glue
- Stiff paper or cellophane

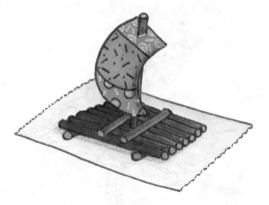

1. Follow the drawing. Line up seven sticks on the wax paper.

2. Squeeze glue between the sticks.

3. Let the glue dry.

4. Lay down two sticks on each end and glue.

5. After the glue dries, turn over the raft and glue down two more sticks.

6. Make a sail by pushing the paper onto the last stick. These will be the mast and sail for sailing.

7. Glue the mast down between one of the cross-sticks and put the last one next to it.

8. Tie the string to one end of the raft so you can keep it from floating away.

More to Try: Decorate your sail. To make the raft look more like a real one, bind the raft sticks with string instead of glue.

TRY IT!

MUSIC

Music is the art of making sounds. Different cultures find different sounds pleasing to the ear. Some sounds in nature, like birdcalls, are musical. You can make your own music.

Move to the Music

Listen to different kinds of music—fast, slow, lots of instruments or voices, one instrument or one voice. Think of a story that goes with the music. Make up movements to tell the story.

Rhythm Instruments

Look at pages 266–268 for directions to make some instruments. Play in your own troop band.

Singing in Rounds

To sing in rounds, groups start singing a song at different times. Practice singing "Make New Friends," page 168. Split into two groups. Group A sings first. When Group A reaches the second line of the song, Group B starts singing. What other songs can be sung in rounds?

Action Songs

Practice the action song on page 24. The "Brownie Smile Song" is an action song. "Bingo," found in the *Sing-Along Songbook*, is another. Do you know any action songs you can share with your friends?

Melody Glasses

Drinking glasses filled with different amounts of water can become a musical instrument. This activity and many other fun ones are in the Contemporary Issues book, *Into the World of Today and Tomorrow: Leading Girls into Mathematics, Science, and Technology.*

Twinkle, twinkle, little star,
  1   1   5   5   6 6   5
How I wonder what you are
  4   4   3   3   2   2   1
Up above the world so high
  5   5   4   4   3   3   2
Like a diamond in the sky.
  5   5   4   4   3   3   2
Twinkle, twinkle, little star
  1   1   5   5   6 6   5
How I wonder what you are.
  4   4   3 3   2   2   1

You will need:

- 8 same-size drinking glasses
- Water
- Spoon

1. Number the glasses from one through eight.

2. Fill each glass with the amount of water shown in the picture.

3. Play "Twinkle, Twinkle, Little Star" on your melody glasses. The numbers tell which glasses to tap. If a note doesn't sound just right, try adding or taking away a little water. Tap fast or slow in different places to follow the rhythm.

Music Around the World

Try singing The "Brownie Friend-Maker Song" from the *Sing-Along Songbook* and cassette. The tune is from Israel. Do you know any songs from different countries you can choose?

Brownie Friend-Maker Song

KAY TEMPLETON   TRADITIONAL ISRAELI

1. Your Brown-ie hand in my Brown-ie hand and
my Brown-ie hand in your Brown-ie hand.
Come a-long with me and sing a-long with me. Yes I'll
come a-long with you and__ sing a-long with you.

Chorus

Hi! Ho! Friend ma-kers all. Hand in hand's the
Brown-ie style. Hi! Ho! Friend ma-kers all.
Greet you with a Brown - ie smile.

Do a grand right and left as you sing.

2. Your Brownie hand in my Brownie hand,
And my Brownie hand in your Brownie hand.
We have Brownie friends in many lands
Across the seven seas, the mountains and the sands.

Chorus:
Hi! Ho! Friend ma-kers all.
Hand in hand's the Brown-ie style.
Hi! Ho! Friend ma-kers all.
Greet you with a Brown-ie smile.

3. Your Brownie hand in my Brownie hand,
And my Brownie hand in your Brownie hand.
On Thinking Day our love goes forth to ev'ry friend,
A chain of Brownie hands reaching out, their help to lend.

Chorus:
Hi! Ho! Friend ma-kers all.
Hand in hand's the Brown-ie style.
Hi! Ho! Friend ma-kers all.
Greet you with a Brown-ie smile.

MY BODY

Try these activities to find out more about your body.

Brain Power

Try these activities to see how your brain works.

Different Muscles

Sit at a table and write your name. Then take one of your feet and move it in a circle on the floor.

Now try doing both things together. Sometimes it's hard for your brain to do two things at once.

Eye to Brain to Hand

Cut a piece of paper the size of a dollar bill. Hold it in front of a friend who has her fingers ready to catch it. Drop it and ask her to try to catch it before it falls to the floor. The eyes send messages to the brain that then tell the hands what to do. But sometimes an object falls faster than messages travel. Try to improve through practice.

Dreams

Your brain works even while you're sleeping—that's why you have dreams. In a circle with friends, tell about one of your dreams.

Fingerprints

Your fingerprints are not like anyone else's. Even identical twins have different fingerprints. Do the fingerprinting activity on page 37. Then make fingerprints of three other people on clean white paper.

Reflexes

Try these activities to test your reflexes.

Eye Changes

In a room with lots of light, sit facing a friend. Watch what happens to the black center part of the eye called the pupil. The colored part of the eye, the iris, is changing with the light. Your body does this automatically.

Knee Jerk

Sit on something that is high enough so that your feet don't touch the floor. Cross your legs. On the top leg, feel your kneecap. Just below your kneecap is a soft spot. Have a friend gently tap this spot with the back of this book.

Muscle Reaction

Make one of your arms very straight. Ask a friend to hold your arm down while you try as hard as you can to lift it. Your friend can use both hands. Count to 20, trying as hard as you can to lift your arm. After you have counted to 20, your friend can let go. Stand still and let your arm relax. What does your arm do?

Pulse

Your heart pumps blood through the body. Every time your heart beats, it pushes a new supply of blood into your arteries (ar-tuh-reez). Arteries are the tubes that carry blood away from your heart. You can feel this as your pulse. The blood then goes into your veins, the tubes that carry the blood back to your heart.

Take your pulse by placing three fingers of the hand you write with on the flat side of your neck. (See the picture.) Hold them still until you feel a slight beating. Now try to feel your pulse in your wrist. Hold your fingers as the diagram shows. You can even watch your pulse. Try this: Put a thumbtack through one end of a wooden match. Rest your arm on a table. Rest the thumbtack with the match on the spot on your wrist where you found your pulse. Watch closely. What happens?

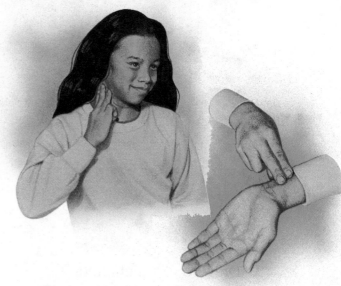

More to Try: Try to find a different spot on your body where you can feel your pulse. Practice taking someone else's pulse.

A Fit Body

Try making a fitness wheel like in the picture and do some of the exercises.

You will need:

- Heavy cardboard
- Scissors
- Crayons or markers

1. Cut a piece of heavy cardboard into a circle.

2. Draw four straight lines through the middle of the circle. Color them different colors, if you want. These will be your eight places to write the names of exercises. Here are some ideas:

- Jumping jacks
- Marching
- Skipping
- Side leg raises
- Hopping
- Sit-ups
- Push-ups
- Waist twists

3. Close your eyes and point to the wheel and do the exercise you picked.

Body Parts

Your body has many parts that work together. Most people have the same parts, but none are just alike. Try this activity to see how you are alike and how you are different.

You will need:

- Butcher paper or other long pieces of paper
- Pencils
- 13 paper fasteners for each girl
- Scissors

1. Choose a partner. Take turns tracing each other's bodies on the paper.

2. Cut around the body that was drawn.

3. Cut the body apart at the neck, shoulders, elbows, wrists, thighs, knees, and ankles (see the picture).

4. Fasten the body parts back together with the paper fasteners. You now have moving body parts, like parts of a puppet.

5. Label the different body parts.

6. Display your "body puppets" around the room.

NUMBERS AND SHAPES

Sailboat at dock

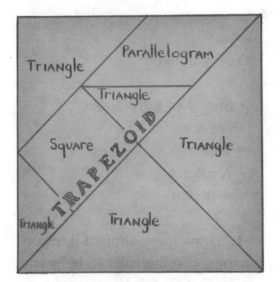

Triangle · Parallelogram · Triangle · Square · TRAPEZOID · Triangle · Triangle · Triangle

Have some fun with numbers and shapes.

Math Shapes

Try to make different patterns from the same shapes.

You will need:

- Paper
- Scissors
- A ruler
- A pencil

1. Have someone help you trace or draw the different shapes inside the square.

2. Cut the paper on the lines.

3. Try to put your shapes back into the same square.

4. Try to make other patterns and designs. You will find out more about shapes, like triangles and rectangles, when you study geometry (gee-om-eh-tree).

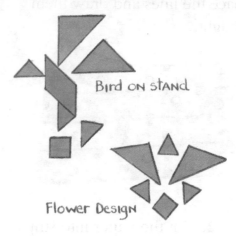

Bird on stand

Flower Design

Mobius Strips

Simple paper magic can happen with Mobius (mo-bee-us) strips. These paper strips are named after the German mathematician August F. Mobius.

You will need:

- Sheets of newspaper
- Scissors
- Tape
- A ruler
- A pencil

1. Draw long, straight lines on the paper. Use the ruler to help you space the lines and draw them straight.

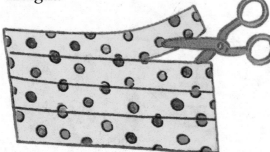

2. Cut the paper into strips along the lines.

3. Make the three different kinds of loops, as shown.

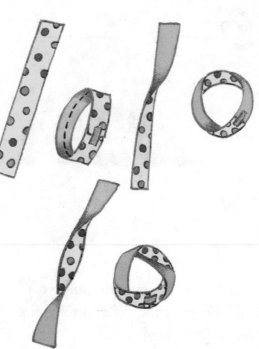

4. Tape the ends.
5. Cut the loops in half.

More twist fun: Make the same kinds of loops as above, but do not cut them in half. Cut one-third of the way in and keep on cutting.

Origami

Origami (ore-ee-gahm-ee) is the Japanese art of folding paper. Try making an origami cat.

You will need a square sheet of paper (you can make a paper rectangle into a square by copying these pictures).

Cat

1. Fold the square to make a triangle. See the picture.

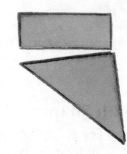

2. Fold the bottom part of the triangle up. This is called a trapezoid (trap-uh-zoyd). See the picture.

3. Fold the right and left points up and to the front. See the picture.

4. What do you have? You can draw a cat's face. Do you know what the shape of the face is called? Hint: It has five sides. What other animals or things can you make by folding paper?

More to Try: Find a book on origami and try making art with other shapes.

Jigsaw Puzzles

Try making your own puzzle. You will need:

- Scissors
- Heavy paper
- Glue or paste
- Newspaper or wax paper
- Books or other heavy things
- A pen
- A picture of something you like
- An envelope

1. Spread a thin coat of glue on the heavy paper.

2. Put your picture on the gluey paper and press it smooth.

3. Dry the paper flat by covering it with newspaper or wax paper and laying books on top. Let the papers dry for one day or more.

4. Trim the edges of your paper.

5. Draw four or five lines over the back of your paper.

6. Cut the paper apart.

7. Try to put your puzzle back together.

8. Store the pieces of your puzzle in an envelope for safekeeping.

More to Try: Trade puzzles with friends. Are some easier to put together than others? What makes a jigsaw puzzle hard to complete?

Time and Money

Read pages 130–132 about time and money in "How and Why?" Try some of the activities.

Nature Shapes

Read pages 153–154 in "How and Why?" Do the activity about looking for different shapes in natural things.

OUTDOOR ADVENTURER

A Hike

Plan a day hike in a forest, park, or nature preserve. Your plan should include clothing, a snack or sack lunch, and safety measures. Use a map of the area when making your plan. Do one of the following activities:

1. Try following a nature trail that leads you on a guided exploration of the area.

2. Try a color hike. Take a box of crayons with you on your hike with at least one color for each person. Try to find things that match the crayon colors.

3. Try one of the hiking activities on pages 153–154.

D oing activities outside is a special part of being a Brownie Girl Scout. Before you do any of the activities below, review the outdoor skills checklist on pages 149–150.

Neighborhood Map

Pretend that you are a bird looking down on the earth. Draw a map of your meeting place, back-yard, or a neighborhood park as you might see it from above. Put in buildings, pathways, plants growing, and other things of interest.

Sleep Out!

Plan for and go on an overnight with your troop in someone's back-yard, a troop camping facility, or a council camp area.

Review your outdoor skills on pages 149–150. Pick an activity from this book to do and a recipe to make.

Camp

Visit your council camp or day-camp area.

Using a Pocket Knife

When using a pocket knife, always be very careful. Always carry the knife closed. Always close the knife before giving it to someone else. You can learn to use a pocket knife by practicing these safety tips:

1. Use both hands to hold the knife.

2. Keep fingers behind the cutting blade edge when opening and closing.

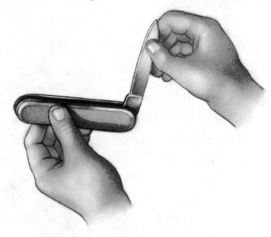

3. Hold the knife like this.

4. Always cut away from your body.

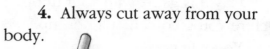

5. Put the knife in a safe place when you are not using it.

Try to peel and cut a carrot into sticks for an outdoor snack.

Dress for the Weather Relay

Play this game with your troop before you go on an outdoor trip. You will need:

- 2 paper bags
- 2 sets of clothes, adult size and for different types of weather

1. Divide into two teams. Pick a starting point and a turnaround point.

2. Have each team form a line behind the starting line. Give each team a bag of clothes.

3. At a signal, one girl from each team puts on the clothes in the bag. She moves as quickly as possible to the turnaround point. She then returns to the starting line, and takes the clothes off and puts them into the bag. She then hands the bag to the next girl in line.

4. This continues until each girl on the team has done the same thing as the first girl. The first team to finish sits down and the members raise their hands.

To make the game even more fun, place clothes for different kinds of weather in one bag. The team has to pick the right clothes for the kind of weather the group decides on.

OUTDOOR FUN

Girl Scouts have always been learning and doing things in the out-of-doors. These activities will help you learn and practice new skills and become an outdoor discoverer.

Trail Signs

Trail signs form shapes that show you which way to go and what to do on a trail. Learn how to make and use the trail signs that are on page 157.

Knots

Knots are very useful in the out-of-doors. Learn how to make the knots on page 159. Read the directions carefully.

Ecology Hunt

"Ecology" (ee-kol-o-gee) is the study of living things—plants and animals—and their environment, their place on earth.

Try to find the things on the list below. Go on a look-and-see hunt. Keep a record of what you find without disturbing anything.

- ☐ 3 kinds of leaves

- ☐ 3 kinds of rocks

- ☐ 3 kinds of plants

- ☐ 3 kinds of insects

- ☐ 3 animals that live in the air

- ☐ 3 animals that live under the ground

- ☐ 3 animals that live in plants or trees

- ☐ 3 things that show an animal has been here

Touch, Smell, Listen

You can learn about the outside world with all your senses. In this hunt, you will use more than your eyes to learn about the out-of-doors. You will need this book and a pencil.

Find the things in the out-of-doors that match the descriptions on this list. Try to find more than one. Try to find things that are not on the list. After you find something, touch it and smell it to find out more about it.

Touch List

☐ Something rough

☐ Something smooth

☐ Something dull

☐ Something pointy

☐ Something soft

☐ Something hard

☐ Something bumpy

☐ Something squishy

☐ Something crumbly

☐ Something wet

Smell List

☐ Something sweet-smelling

☐ Something sour-smelling

☐ Something flowery

☐ Something minty

☐ Something bad-smelling

☐ Something pinelike

☐ Something lemony

☐ Something fruity

Listen List

☐ Leaves rustling

☐ Birds singing

☐ Birds flying

☐ Animals moving

☐ Water running

☐ Insects chirping

☐ Wind moving things

Rubbings

A rubbing is one way to bring home something from the out-of-doors without disturbing nature. Check the lists at right to see which are good and not good to use for rubbings:

You will need:
- Crayons
- Plain white paper

1. Lay your paper against the thing you want to rub.

2. Gently rub a crayon back and forth until a pattern starts to show.

3. Do any of your rubbing patterns look alike? Try to collect many different patterns.

4. Show your rubbings to others. See if they can guess what your rubbings are.

Good

☐ Tree bark ☐ Flat stones

☐ Leaves ☐ Pine needles

☐ Sand ☐ Large rocks

Not Good

☐ Living creatures

☐ Flowers

☐ Very soft things

Outdoor Snacks

On pages 154–155 and 156 in "How and Why?" you learned to make a fruit-and-nut mix and a walking salad. Find a cookbook that has other healthy recipes for foods that can be kept safe without a cooler. Make one to take on your next outdoor trip.

TRY IT!

OUTDOOR HAPPENINGS

It is fun to see how and why things happen outdoors. Try these activities to learn more about outdoor happenings like seed sprouts in the spring and morning dew.

Water Evaporator

Read page 138 and try the water evaporation activity.

Watching Rain and What it Does

Read the section on clouds and rain on page 139. Make a rain gauge using the directions on page 140.

Fossil Prints

Fossils are the prints that animals and plants left in soft mud a very long time ago.

Try this to see how prints that are made on soft, wet mud can harden.

You will need:

- Plaster of Paris
- A 2″ deep tray made from the bottom of a milk carton
- Something to imprint (leaf, feather, piece of bark, etc., you can even use your hand!)

1. Have someone help you mix the plaster and fill the container. Be careful not to make the plaster too wet.

2. Lay the thing that you are going to imprint on the moist plaster.

3. Gently press on the whole piece and leave it for one and a half minutes.

4. Lift it carefully and leave the plaster to dry.

5. Compare your imprint with others.

Seed Race

Seeds take different amounts of time to grow. Try this experiment to see which seed wins a sprout race.

You will need:

- Potting soil
- 6 kinds of seeds
- 1/2 of an egg carton
- Spoon
- Water

Fill each section of the egg carton with about two tablespoons of potting soil. Put one kind of seed in each section. Label each section. Cover the seeds with soil and sprinkle with water. Add some water every day. Which seed sprouts first? Try planting your sprouted seeds outside.

Which Way Does the Wind Blow?

Read about the wind and what it does on page 138. Go out on three different days and watch the wind. You can do it more easily by making your own weather vane. Here is a simple one you can try.

You will need:

- Large paper cup
- Clay
- Pencil with eraser
- Pin
- Straw
- Heavy cardboard
- Index cards or construction paper
- Tape
- Compass (optional)

1. Make a hole in the middle of the bottom of the cup and push the pencil in.

2. Use the clay to make the cup stick to the heavy cardboard.

3. Cut two small triangles from the index card or construction paper. Connect one to each end of the straw.

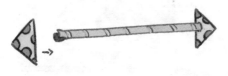

4. Push the pin through the middle of the straw and into the eraser.

5. Take the weather vane outside and put it on a flat surface. Use the compass to mark north, south, east, and west on the cup. If you do not have a compass, use the sun as your guide. It rises in the east and sets in the west.

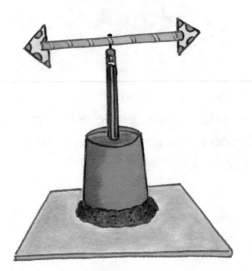

Rocks

In the out-of-doors, you can find many kinds of rocks. Some are formed by mud and sand and other hardening things. They are "sedimentary" (said-ah-men-ta-ree) rocks. Try this experiment to see how they form.

You will need:

- Pebbles
- Sand
- Pieces of rock
- Dirt
- Plaster of Paris
- Water
- A paper cup

1. Have someone help you mix the plaster in the paper cup. Make one-half cup.

2. Measure one teaspoon of pebbles, sand, dirt, and rock pieces.

3. Stir these into the plaster.

4. Let the plaster mix dry.
5. Peel away the paper cup.

6. See if you can find a natural rock that looks like the one you made.

PEOPLE OF THE WORLD

Try these activities to learn more about people.

Language Hunt

Look through this book. How many different languages can you find in this book? Hint: Not all the languages in this book are spoken. How many languages are spoken in your community?

Brownie Girl Scouts in Other Countries

Learn about Brownie Girl Scouts in different countries. Read the chapter "People Near and Far" and do two of the activities.

Games of the World

Look through this book. Find some games from other countries. Learn them well enough to teach them to others.

Songs

Look in your school or local library for some tapes or books of songs from other countries. Try learning a new song.

Prejudice Fighter

Read pages 109–110 about prejudice and do the role-play activities.

World Stories

Close your eyes and put your finger on a globe or world map. Use your imagination and tell a story about a girl your age who lives there.

PAPUA NEW GUINEA

TRY IT!
PLANTS

Adopt a Tree

Adopt a tree by choosing a tree to care for near your home or in your neighborhood. Keep a record of the tree's growth, if possible, and observe how it changes during the seasons. What did you learn about your tree? Share this with other girls in your troop.

Plants have many uses—lumber, paper, medicine, food—and plants make oxygen part of the air you breathe.

Seed Sprout

Sprinkle some alfalfa seeds on two damp sponges. Put one in a dark place and one in a sunny place.

Keep them damp. What happens to the seeds?

Supermarket Plant Hunt

Plants are the beginning of the food chain, even for people. Visit a market or grocery store. Find at least five different plants or plant products that you normally do not eat. Find out how to prepare them and try them. Try preparing an all-plant meal with your Brownie Girl Scout troop or group.

Leaf Hunt

Look for different types of leaves that have fallen to the ground. (Don't put your hands in your mouth after touching leaves and never put any leaves in your mouth. Be sure to wash your hands when you are done.) Pick one leaf that you like a lot. Describe it by drawing it or writing about it. You and your friends can put all your leaves in a pile. Describe your leaf to someone. Can she find it?

Food Chain

Plants make food for all living things and use the sun's energy to grow. When animals eat plants, they get energy. You get energy from eating food. Your food may be from plants or animals. A food chain shows how food energy is passed from one living thing to another. All food chains start with plant life. You can make your own food chain with this activity.

You will need:

- Paper the size of this page, cut in half the long way
- Crayons or markers
- Pencils
- Tape
- Pictures of plants and animals

1. Find a picture of a plant, or draw one. Tape it to a strip of paper.

2. With a piece of tape, loop the ends of the paper together. You now have the first link in your food chain.

3. Find or draw a picture of something that can eat your plant. Tape this to a new strip of paper. Loop the strip through the first link and tape the ends. Now your food chain has two links.

4. Find or draw a picture of something that can eat your second link, and make a third loop as in Step 3.

5. Keep going. Here are some food chain ideas for you to start with:

Corn—insect—small bird— fox.

Acorn—squirrel—hawk.

Flower—beetle—skunk—great horned owl.

Plankton—water insect— frog—fish—bigger fish— heron.

Simple Plants

Mold is a very simple plant that makes spores. Spores are like very small seeds. They are in the air and in dust. Try making some mold.

Wet a folded paper towel with water. Wave some bread in the air or sprinkle it with dust. Put the bread on the towel, wrap it in foil, and put it in a dark spot. Check the bread every day. Rewrap it after checking. Use a toothpic to move the bread and  wash your hands each time. Keep a record of what you see. A magnifying glass can help.

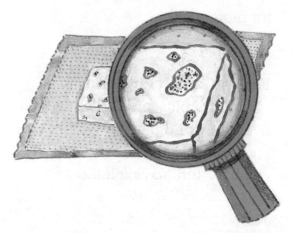

PLAY

People all over the world have ways to relax and play. Here are some games for you to try that children in many countries play. Look in *Games for Girl Scouts* for more ideas.

Kim's Game (England)

Girl Scouts and Girl Guides all over the world play this game. You and your Brownie Girl Scout friends can have fun playing it too!

You will need:

- 1 or more friends
- At least 10 small things
- A scarf

1. Put ten things on a table. Be sure you can cover all of them with the scarf.

2. Show the players the ten things for one minute. Then cover them with the scarf.

3. Ask the players what was on the table. See if they can list all ten things.

Red Light, Green Light (United States of America)

Here is one of many ways to play this game.

1. Choose someone to be It. The person who is It stands at one end of the playing field, far away from all the other players.

2. The others line up along the starting line at the other end of the field.

3. It turns her back to the group and yells "green light." The players may now run toward It.

4. When It yells "red light," everyone must stop running and freeze. It turns around right after she yells "red light." If It catches anyone moving, that person has to go back to the starting line.

5. The game continues until someone has been able to reach and touch It while It has her back turned to the group.

6. That person becomes It.

Sheep and Hyena (Sudan)

See if you can keep the sheep away from the hungry hyena! Get at least ten people to play—more are even better!

1. Players join hands and form a tight circle.

2. One player stays outside the circle. She is the hyena.

3. Another player stays inside the circle. She is the sheep.

4. The players in the circle have to try to keep the hyena from breaking through the circle to get to the sheep. The game ends when the hyena gets the sheep or gets too tired to go after the sheep anymore.

5. Two other people become the sheep and hyena.

Jan-Ken-Pon (Japan)

This is a fun game played in Japan. Look on page 101 to find out how to play it. Teach it to someone else.

Mr. Bear (Sweden)

The moral of this game is "Watch out for sleeping bears!" Look on page 101 to find out how to play this game.

Hawk and Hens (Zimbabwe)

This is a great chasing game for times when you have lots of energy and want to run. See page 101 to learn how to play. Try teaching it to some younger children.

PUPPETS, DOLLS, AND PLAYS

You know about many kinds of art. Did you know that making puppets and dolls is an art? You can use them in plays or stories.

Finger Puppets

Turn the fingers of the gloves into little puppets. Then put on a play.

You will need:

- An old cloth or knitted glove
- Piece of ribbon
- String
- Thread
- Yarn
- Glue
- Scraps of old material
- Markers
- Small buttons
- Beads
- Tissue paper

1. Make five grape-sized balls with the tissue paper, and stuff one into each finger of the glove.

2. Tie a piece of ribbon or yarn under the tissue ball.

3. Put a face on the fingertip with the markers, or sew or glue on buttons or beads.

4. Glue threads or yarn on the tip of the finger for hair.

5. Use yarn and scraps of cloth to dress your puppet.

6. Play with your finger puppets.

Yarn Doll

These dolls are easy to make.
You can add your own ideas.
You will need:

- Yarn or heavy thread
- A small Ping-Pong ball, a small round pebble, or a small ball of yarn
- Ribbons
- Cloth scraps
- Buttons
- Other materials you like

1. Cut yarn into strips the length of this page.

2. Make enough strips to fill your hand.

3. Tie all the strips together at the top.

4. Insert a Ping-Pong ball, pebble, or small ball of yarn to give shape to the head.

5. Tie another string to the bottom of the ball, pebble, or ball of yarn to make a neck.

6. Make arms and legs and a waist, like in the drawing.

7. Use cloth and ribbons to dress the doll.

Paper-Bag Puppet

These puppets are easy to make. They are especially good if you want to make an animal puppet.

You will need:

- Small paper bags
- Pieces of paper
- Crayons
- Markers or paint
- Scissors
- Glue

1. Place the paper bag flat on a table with the bottom fold on top.

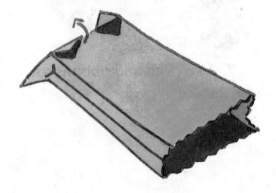

2. Draw and color designs on the bottom fold of the bag. This will be the head of your puppet. You can add eyes, ears, and hair.

3. Decorate the rest of the bag. What did you make?

Safety Play

Read about safety on pages 48–57. Create a puppet show about safety do's and don'ts.

A Puppet Stage

A stage will make a puppet show much more fun. A puppet stage will have three parts—the stage itself, a curtain, and scenery.

Try using a box, a table, chairs, and a sheet, a towel, or tablecloth for the stage and curtain. What can you use for scenery? Look around your home or meeting place, or cut out some shapes from heavy cardboard.

Marionette

There are string puppets as well as hand puppets. String puppets are called "marionettes." You can make them move around just like you do! Try making this marionette.

You will need:

- Cardboard
- String
- Beads or buttons
- A stick or dowel
- Crayons or paints
- Paper
- Glue
- A big needle
- Heavy thread

1. Cut the cardboard into an animal or human shape. Make a head, body, arms, and legs.

2. Color the pieces.

3. With the needle, poke four holes in the body for the arms and legs. Then poke a hole at the top of each arm and leg.

4. Thread the needle and use it to tie together each leg and arm to the body.

5. Make a hole for the head at the top of the body.

6. Attach the head to the body by threading the hole. Tie a knot and cut the string.

7. Tie another string to the top of the head. To make your puppet move, raise and lower it by holding the string.

OR

8. Tie a string to each arm and leg. Then tie these strings to two sticks tied in a cross.

9. Make your marionette walk and dance by moving the sticks.

SAFETY

Every Girl Scout knows the motto, "Be Prepared." Read pages 48–57 about safety and try these activities.

Street Safety

Being safe on the street is just as important as keeping yourself safe at home. To be safe on the street, you should get to know your neighborhood. Try these two activities to learn more about your neighborhood.

1. Take a walk through your neighborhood with an adult you trust. Look for street names, the firehouse, and the police station. Look at the people around you.

2. Make a map of your neighborhood and mark the places you need to know about to stay safe.

Fire Safety

Read the section on fire safety on pages 54–56. Find out about the fire escape plan for your Brownie Girl Scout meeting place and practice it.

A fire escape plan is important, but it is not the only part of fire safety. A fire can start at night or during the day, and being alert to the danger is the first step to help get you and your family out alive. Try this fire safety activity.

1. Learn what a smoke alarm is and how it works. If there is no smoke alarm in your home, go with an adult in your family to a hardware store. Have an employee explain why smoke alarms are necessary in everyone's home.

2. Have an adult test the smoke alarm so you can hear what it sounds like.

Playground Safety

A playground should be a place where you can enjoy good and healthy fun and exercise. But if you don't use playground equipment correctly, it can be dangerous. Learn the rules of playground safety and share them with others before you have an accident.

1. Make up some rules for playgrounds. Use these rules to make safety posters to put up in your playground and troop meeting place.

2. Look at the equipment in the playground at your school or in your neighborhood. With an adult, give the equipment a safety check. Are the swings anchored well? Is the slide stable? Make notes about unsafe equipment and show them to the proper officials.

First Aid

Sometimes you may be the only one around when somebody needs help. Learn a skill that could save a life in an emergency. One skill that is good to know is how to save a person who is choking. Many people do choke while eating. You can tell if a person is in trouble if she can't talk, if she points to her mouth, or if she is turning blue. With an adult, try this exercise on first aid for choking.

1. To find your rib cage, use your left hand, make a fist, and place it over your belly button. Then, using your right hand, make a fist and place it on top of your left fist. This spot is just below the rib cage and is important to find when you are doing first aid on a person who is choking.

2. With a partner, practice the following, but be sure when you're practicing not to push hard on the person's stomach.

Pretend your partner is choking. Keep her calm. Ask if she is all right. Ask her to cough. If she cannot breathe, cough, or speak:

- Stand behind her.
- Use your left hand to make a fist and place it over her belly button.
- Use your right hand to make a fist and place it on top of the left fist. Remove your left hand. Then cover your right fist with your left hand.
- Then push your fist in and up quickly.
- Keep doing this until she can cough, breathe, or speak.

More to Try: Practice first aid for choking on yourself in case there is a time when no one can help you. See the pictures in the center column.

More to Try: Practice the other first-aid skills on pages 58–62.

Safety Center

Make a place to keep information you'll need in an emergency. You will need:

- A hanger
- A large piece of fabric
- Scissors
- A stapler or a needle and thread
- Markers
- At least 4 legal-sized envelopes

1. Cut the fabric into a large square.

2. Wrap one end of the fabric around the hanger and staple or sew it with a needle and thread as shown.

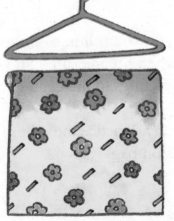

3. With a marker, label the envelopes. A few ideas are:

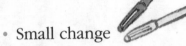

- Small change
- Emergency phone numbers
- Reminder notes

Include an envelope in which to keep paper and a pencil for taking messages.

4. Staple or sew each envelope to the fabric as shown. Have someone hang it near the phone for you to reach easily.

Suzy Safety Says

Can you find all the Suzy Safety pictures in this handbook? Suzy Safety is asking you to do things the safe way. Every time you see her picture, remember the safety rules you have learned.

TRY IT!

SCIENCE IN ACTION

Science is a part of our daily life. Science is in action when you use machines, tell time, go to the doctor, or grow a plant. Did you know that even making bread uses science? It uses chemistry (kem-is-tree). This Try-It will help you see science in action.

Computer Fun Fair

Organize or participate in a computer fun fair. Find a computer that you and your friends can use. Have people in your troop bring computer games to a meeting and try them, or visit a store that carries computer games and have an employee give you a demonstration. Decide what to look for in a good computer game.

Energy Sleuth

Think of the kinds of energy that you use daily. Do you use electricity? Do you use gas or oil? Do you use solar energy or thermal power? Keep a record of the times you use some form of energy, other than your own power, for a full day. Look closely at your list. Are there any ways that you can save energy each day? Find at least three ways and try them for a week.

More to Try: Create a poster or sign to help family members or friends at school conserve energy in some way.

Make a Color Spectrum

Try the color spectrum activity on pages 136–137.

Computers in Your Life

Use a computer at home or at school to solve a problem, check your spelling, write a story, or learn something new.

OR

Talk to three people who use computers at work. Find out what they do and what kind of help and information they get from their computers. Ask them how they learned to use a computer. Tell others what you learned.

Time Check

Read about time on page 130. Look for different ways of telling time. Try making the hourglass on pages 130–131 in "How and Why?"

Bread Making

All sorts of things happen when you make a loaf of yeast bread. Yeast is really millions of tiny one-celled plants that start to grow when you add water or milk. Without the yeast, your bread would not have all those wonderful air spaces that make it light and fluffy. Many of the things we cook depend on chemistry between ingredients to get to the finished product.

 This is a great activity for a rainy day. Be sure to do it with an adult. Make sure you measure carefully.

You will need:

- A kitchen with an oven and these items:
- 1 package or cake of yeast
- 2 cups of lukewarm milk
- 2 tablespoons of sugar
- 1 tablespoon of salt
- 6 cups of flour
- 5 tablespoons of butter or margarine, melted
- A large mixing bowl
- A wooden spoon
- 2 loaf pans
- A small pan for melting butter
- A kitchen towel
- A pot holder

1. Wash your hands. Put all of your materials out so that you can get to them easily.

2. Place the two cups of lukewarm milk into your bowl. Warm the milk slightly if it has been in the refrigerator.

3. Add the yeast and sugar and salt. Stir with the wooden spoon so the yeast dissolves.

4. Add the flour a little bit at a time, and stir it with the wooden spoon. When it gets too hard to stir with the spoon, add the melted butter or margarine. Use the spoon to mix it in. Keep adding the flour until it is used up. By this time you may want to use your hands (be sure they are clean) to mix the dough.

5. The dough should look smooth and be stretchable. Now you get to knead the dough. Sprinkle flour on a wooden breadboard or on your kitchen counter. Then pour the dough onto this surface. This is called "turning it out." Fold the dough toward you, then push away in a rocking motion with the heels of your hands, eight to ten times. Turn the dough a one-quarter turn and do it again. Take turns if you

are doing this as a group. Knead for about five to ten minutes.

6. When you are finished kneading, shape your dough into a nice big ball and put it in the mixing bowl again. Cover it with a towel and place it in a warm spot in the kitchen, away from drafts.

7. Now comes the easy part. You have to wait for an hour and a half to two hours for the chemical reaction to take place. You should let the dough grow until it is double its original size. What is happening here? The yeast plants are reacting with the sugar and produce carbon dioxide, which is a gas. When the bread dough is warmed, the carbon dioxide gas bubbles grow larger and cause the dough to rise.

8. After your dough has grown to twice its size, it is time to punch it. What happens when you punch it hard two or three times? Sprinkle some flour on your breadboard or table and take your dough out to

knead it for about three or four minutes.

9. Divide your dough into two equal parts. Coat the inside of your loaf pans with butter or vegetable oil. Mold each portion of dough into the shape of the pan and put it in the loaf pan. Cover the loaf pans with the towel and put them in a warm place. The loaves should double in size again.

10. When your loaves are doubled in size, pop them in the oven at a temperature of 375° F. Bake for around 45 minutes or until the loaves are a nice golden brown. Remove the loaves from the oven with a pot holder. Cool the loaves before removing them from the pan. Eat the bread while it is still warm.

When you cut the bread, look at the texture. During the baking, the carbon dioxide bubbles have continued to grow and have made those air spaces. All the better for butter and jam!

TRY IT!

SCIENCE WONDERS

Try these activities to see how wonderful science is. The changes seem like magic, but a scientist can make them happen. And you get to be the scientist!

Home-Grown Crystals

Crystals are minerals that are clear and sparkly. Some crystals have colors, too! Ice, salt, and diamonds are all crystals. So is rock candy! Try growing some of your own crystals with this experiment.

You will need:
- Jar
- Hot water
- 1 cup of sugar
- Clean string
- Pencil
- Paper clip

1. Fill the jar with one-half cup of hot water.

2. Add the cup of sugar.

3. Wrap one end of a piece of string around the pencil. Knot it.

4. Put the pencil across the top of the jar and let the other end of the string hang almost to the bottom.

Use the paper clip to keep it down.

5. Let it sit for a few days. Then you can eat your experiment!

More to Try: Look for crystals outdoors. Many rocks have crystals. A magnifying glass will help you see them.

Bubbles

You can make some special bubbles. Try this mix.

- 1 gallon water
- 40 drops of glycerine
- ½ cup dishwashing liquid

Mix together in a large flat pan. Stir slowly. If you can, let it set for at least one day. The glycerine can make stronger bubbles.

For your bubble maker, have an adult help you shape a metal hanger. Dip your bubble maker into the pan and then gently wave it in the air. Try other shapes for your bubble makers.

Homemade Recycled Paper

A fun recycling activity is making your own paper. You can make paper for books, posters, newsletters, paintings, and many other things.

You will need:

- A large mixing bowl
- An eggbeater
- A cup
- A big spoon
- An old newspaper
- Water
- A screen about 3″ square or bigger
- A flat pan a little larger than the screen
- Starch

1. Tear a half-page of news-

paper into very small pieces. Put the paper in a large mixing bowl full of water.

2. Let the paper soak for one hour.

3. Beat the paper with an eggbeater for ten minutes. The paper should be soft and mushy. It is now called "pulp."

4. Mix two tablespoons of starch in one cup of water. Add this to the pulp. Stir well. The starch makes the paper pulp strong.

5. Pour the pulp into the flat pan.

6. Place the screen in the bottom of the pan. It will become evenly covered with pulp.

7. Put the rest of the newspaper on a table. Pick up the screen covered with pulp and put it on one half of the newspaper.

10. When it is dry, peel your recycled paper from the screen.

8. Fold the other half of the newspaper over the top of the screen. Press down very hard.

9. Fold back the newspaper so you can see the pulp. Let it dry overnight.

Chemistry Magic

Try this experiment to see how new things are formed through chemical reactions.

You will need:

- 5 tablespoons pure laundry soap
- 2 cups warm tap water
- 4 tablespoons salt
- A large glass
- A large spoon for stirring
- 2 one-cup measuring cups

1. Put the laundry soap into one cup of water. Stir until the soap has dissolved.

2. Next, put the salt into another cup of water and stir until the salt is dissolved as much as possible.

3. Pour the soap solution into a large glass. Then pour the salt solution on top of it. Mix well.

What happens? You should see the soap harden and turn into a ball right away. If you let the mixture stand still for a few minutes, the soap will rise to the top and the bottom will stay clear.

Magnet Hunt

Magnets can pull things to them. Most magnets are made of iron and come in many different shapes. Not everything will stick to a magnet. Get a magnet and find out what will stick to it.

1. Take your magnet and touch it to as many different things as you can find.

2. Write down all the things that are pulled to the magnet and all those that are not.

Static Electricity

A special kind of electricity, called static electricity, can be made by rubbing some things together. Lightning is a kind of static electricity in the clouds. The spark you sometimes feel when you touch something after walking on a rug is static electricity. You can try making it now with these activities.

You will need:

• Balloons
• String
• Very small pieces of paper
• Wool cloth

A. **1.** Blow up the balloons and tie the ends.

2. Make static electricity by rubbing a balloon very quickly on the wool cloth. You can use your hair instead of the wool cloth.

3. Hold the balloon over the very small pieces of paper to see static electricity in action.

B. **1.** Take two more balloons and tie a piece of string to each one.

2. Rub the balloons on the wool cloth.

3. Hold the balloons by the string and try to make them touch.

C. **1.** Rub another balloon on the wool cloth.

2. Hold the balloon next to a thin stream of water from a faucet. What happens?

3. Hold this balloon to the wall. If it has enough static electricity, it will stick. Rub the balloon to give it more static charges.

SENSES

You learn about your world in many ways. Seeing, hearing, feeling, smelling, and tasting are the five senses that send messages to your brain about the world around you. You use your senses almost all the time, even when you don't know it!

Only the Nose Knows

Your sense of smell can be very helpful. For example, if food smells bad you probably won't eat it. How is your sense of smell?

You will need:
- A paper or foam egg carton
- A bandanna for a blindfold
- Some paper and tape
- Some "smelly" items

You might start with the following: cinnamon powder, lemon peel, pepper, clove powder, nutmeg, chili powder, garlic powder, soap, toothpaste, or baby powder. You might ask an adult to help you find more spices from the kitchen or other things with strong smells.

1. Break apart the egg carton into separate little cups.

2. Put a small amount of different things to smell in each cup. Write on a small piece of paper what each smell is and attach it to a cup.

3. Blindfold a friend. Have her guess what each smell is, using only her nose. Check her answers by reading the papers.

Making a Better Ear

Many animals depend upon their sense of hearing to find dinner or avoid being eaten for dinner. Do you ever wish that you could hear better? Let's see if you can make a better ear.

For this activity you are going to need:
- A loud ticking clock
- Paper plates
- Construction paper
- Newspaper
- Paper cups
- Cardboard rolls from the middle of paper towels
- Scissors
- String
- Glue

(If you want to decorate your ears you will need crayons, markers, or paints.)

Design a pair of ears that will hear the ticking of the clock before anyone else. Should they be small or should they be large? Should they be long or should they be short? Try it!

When you are ready to test your ears, have someone take the ticking clock across the room. Close your eyes and listen with your ears. You might want to turn your body so that your ears face the direction of the clock. The person with the clock will move closer to you. As soon as you hear the clock ticking, raise your hand and sit down. May the best ears win! Talk about what you have learned from this activity with the rest of the group. Can you find some pictures of animals that have ears like the ones that you made?

Now You See It

Do you always see what is really there? Try this activity that can fool your senses. Make a toy that uses your eyes to trick you. If you close your eyes tight, what do you see? You will see the last thing you were looking at.

You will need:

- A piece of heavy paper or light cardboard that is cut into a 2″ square
- Markers or crayons
- A pencil
- Some tape

1. Hold the paper so that it looks like a diamond, not a square. On one side draw a fishbowl, without the fish, in the middle of the paper.

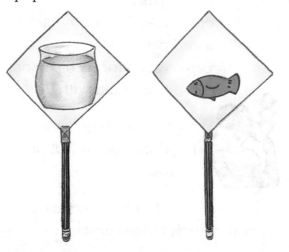

2. On the other side of the paper, draw a fish. Place your fish on the paper so that if you hold your paper up to the light, the fish would be swimming in the fishbowl. (See illustration.)

3. Tape your paper onto the pencil point, with the bottom of the diamond on the top of the pencil tip.

4. Hold the pencil between your hands in an upright position. Roll the pencil back and forth so the paper flips back and forth. Look at the paper. Where is the fish? Why do you think it is there?

Can You Feel It?

Your sense of touch helps you find things in the dark, tell hot from cold, and enjoy warm hugs. Insects have antennae to help them feel their way around. You have hands. For this activity you will need two large paper bags and two of everything else. Pick objects that are the same, or identical, like two sponges, two dried beans, two mittens, two pennies, two rubber bands, two spoons. Make sure you  do not pick anything sharp. Put one of each thing into each of the paper bags. Shake the bags up, then reach into each bag without looking. Can you find the matching objects using only your sense of touch?

Mapping the Tongue

Think about the different kinds of tastes there are when you eat. Mmmmmmm. Tastes can be sweet, salty, sour, or bitter. When you taste something, does your whole tongue taste it? Find out how and where you taste things by making a map of your tongue.

You will need (for each person doing the activity):

- 4 small dishes or plastic film canisters
- Sugar, vinegar, salt
- Unsweetened grapefruit juice
- 4 cotton-tipped swabs
- Sheet of paper
- 4 different-colored crayons or colored pencils
- A cup of water for each person to rinse her mouth with

 Safety tip: Do not share the dishes or the cotton swabs.

1. Place one teaspoon of each of the substances, sugar (sweet), vinegar (sour), salt, and grapefruit juice (bitter) into a different dish or canister. Add a little water to each of the first three.

2. Draw a big letter "U" onto your paper. This is your tongue map.

3. Dip a cotton swab into the sweet solution. Touch it to at least four different parts of your tongue. Wherever you taste sweet, mark it on your tongue map in one color of crayon.

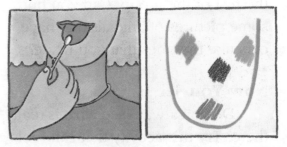

4. Rinse out your mouth very well with water. Use a different cotton swab and a different solution to do the next parts of your map for salty, bitter, and sour. Rinse between each solution.

5. You now have a map of your tongue's taste buds. Does your tongue taste the same flavors in the same spot? Where does your tongue taste sweetness, saltiness, sourness, bitterness?

6. Compare your map with another girl's map. Are they the same?

What's It Like?

What is it like to be missing one of your senses? How do you communicate if you cannot hear? People who cannot hear often use sign language to communicate with others. Learn how to sign your name using the sign alphabet on page 78 or learn how to say the Girl Scout Promise in American Sign Language (see pictures at right).

Girl   Scout   Promise

On   my   honor   I   will   try

to   serve   God   country   help   people

at all times   and   live   Girl   Scout   Law

TRY IT!

SOUNDS OF MUSIC

What makes music different from any other noise? If you think about it, some noises, such as the drip, drip, drip of a faucet, can sound like music. What other noises inside or outside can sound like music? Count one-and-two-and-three-and-four. Or one-one-two-two-three-three-four-four, or one-and-two and one-and-two. Music is different from noise because it usually has a regular sound, or rhythm. Can you make some instruments to make your own rhythms?

Make Your Own

Percussion instruments make a sound when hit or shaken. They can be drums, rattles, gongs, tambourines, or shakers. Try making a shaker, using a paper plate, dry beans, or other small things that rattle, and a stapler. Place the beans on the paper plate, fold in half and staple plate halves to close. Make one for each hand. See page 226 for some other ideas.

Single String Swing

Can one string make music? It can if it's a one-stringed bass fiddle. Try your hand at this one:
You will need:

- A large empty can (#10 size or 48 ounces) that is open at one end
- A nail
- A hammer
- A heavy string
- A pencil

1. Ask an adult to help you use the hammer and nail to punch a hole in the middle of the can bottom.

2. Measure and cut a length of string that goes from the floor to the middle of your thigh.

3. Knot the end of your string. Pull the other end through the inside of the can and through the hole you made. Make sure the knot is big enough so that it keeps the string from pulling all the way through.

4. Tie the other end around the middle of a pencil.

5. To play your instrument, place one foot firmly on the floor and the other foot on the top of the can. Pull the string straight up from the floor so that it is stretched tight with one hand. Now, pluck or jerk the string with the forefinger of the other hand. Experiment with your fiddle sound by plucking in different places on the string. Try holding the string tighter or looser. How does the sound change? Can you get different sounds by changing the length of the string?

Sliding Air

What does wind have to do with music? Different sounds, or notes, are made by changing the amount of air in a tube. If you haven't seen a slide trombone, find a picture of one before doing this activity.

You will need:

- A straw
- Water
- A plastic soda bottle

1. Fill the soda bottle about three-fourths full with water.

2. Place the straw in the water and blow across the straw.

3. Lower the bottle or lift the straw and continue to blow. What happens? What is happening to the air in the straw as you slide it up in the water and as you slide it down? How does that affect the sound? When is the sound the highest? When is it lowest?

Blowing Air

Make a simple wind instrument with a straw. This instrument will have two wedges at one end, called reeds, which lie inside your mouth. The reeds open and close allowing air into the straw. The moving air makes the sound.

You will need:

- A paper straw
- Scissors

You may need an adult's help to cut the triangles.

1. Pinch and flatten a straw about one-half inch to three-fourths inch to the end. Cut off triangles as shown in the diagram. (If you use a plastic straw, you need to flatten the end carefully.)

2. Cut small holes that can be covered by your fingers about one inch apart, about two inches from the other end of the straw, as shown.

3. Put the straw into your mouth so that your lips do not touch the corners of the straw.

4. Blow hard. Do not crunch the straw. Cover one, then two, then three of the small holes. You can play simple tunes by covering the different holes.

Do not march or run with the straw in your mouth!

More to Try: Create a horn by putting a funnel in the end of a length of rubber hose. (Do not cut your garden hose up!) Put your lips tightly together and blow through them into the hose. Guess what moves?

Yahoo, a Kazoo

A kazoo is another instrument that works by moving air. Your mouth can help make the sound.

You will need:

- A cardboard tube from paper or aluminum foil
- A piece of wax paper
- Some tape

1. Stretch the wax paper tightly over one end of the tube. While holding it tight, get someone to help you tape the wax paper to the end, as shown at right.

2. Near the end of the tube with no wax paper, poke a small hole with a pencil so that air can escape.

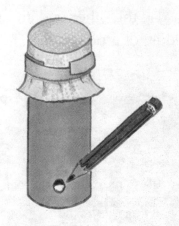

3. Play your kazoo by humming your tune into the tube. Do not sing, but hum "du-du-du."

Strike Up the Band

Try making your own band with your new instruments. Can you make up your own songs? Can you play a song you already know? Try giving a performance for others.

More to Try: Attend a concert put on by a band or orchestra, or view a video of a concert. Can you find instruments that are like the ones you made?

SPACE EXPLORER

Learning about what you see in the sky can be fun. It may be your first step in exploring space. Scientists, astronomers, and astronauts use telescopes, satellites, spaceships, and other scientific equipment to study space.

The Night Sky

Go stargazing with someone who knows the planets and the stars, or have someone help you read a star map. Try to find the North Star, the Big Dipper, the Milky Way, or other constellations. Look for planets and satellites overhead. Perhaps you will even see a meteor or a meteor shower.

The Moon

Why does the moon look like it changes shape? The moonlight you see is the sun shining on one side of the moon. When the earth and moon move around the sun, you see the moon in different places. You also see the parts of the moon that get sunlight. Draw the moon on the same day of the week for four weeks. What did you see?

Ready, Set, Jet!

Pretend that you are on a journey to a Girl Scout center on the moon. How would you dress for space? How would you move in space? Find a way to show what you would wear on your journey. Show your drawing to others. Be ready to answer questions about your space outfit.

Shadow Time

Did you know that the earth rotates? It turns around much like a top. Have you seen the sun in different places in the sky? It looks like the sun is moving, but the earth is moving. Try this activity to mark the earth's movement.

1. Take a stick or stake and put it in the ground. Notice that it casts a shadow. Find the very end of the shadow and mark it with another stick or rock.

2. Leave your markers in the ground and return in an hour. Has something changed? Mark where your shadow is now. Do this once more in another hour. Which way did your shadow move? Did the stick move? What do you think moved to make your shadow move?

More to Try: Keep track of the shadow's movement over several hours. Is there a way you could use this movement to tell time? Visit a sundial in a park or learn how to make one to tell time. Learn how to find which way is north by where the sun is in the sky.

Space Sleuth

Make a model rocket. You can make a very simple rocket that will give you an understanding of rockets that are used to explore space. Try making this balloon rocket to see how.

You will need:

- A large balloon
- Tape
- A plastic straw
- 6 feet or more of string

1. Wet the string and pull it straight.

2. Tie each end of the string to something—a chair, for example.

3. Stretch the string straight.

4. Blow up the balloon and hold the opening closed.

5. Tape the balloon to the straw.

6. Let go of the balloon.

7. Air leaving the balloon pushes against the air in the room, and the balloon moves forward.

OR

Visit a museum or planetarium that has an exhibit or program on space or the stars. If there are none in your community, visit a library to find books on stars and space. Share something you have learned with another person.

Star Maker

Learn about several constellations in the night sky. Pick one and find out how it got its name. Use the pattern of your constellation to make your own indoor star show!

You will need:

- A cylinder-shaped oatmeal or grits container
- A flashlight
- A large safety pin

1. Draw your constellation on the bottom of the cylinder-shaped container on the inside (or draw it backwards on the outside of the box). Mark where the stars are in the constellation. Punch holes in the box very carefully to form your constellation.

2. At night or in a darkened room, place the flashlight in the box and shine it on a blank wall or on the ceiling.

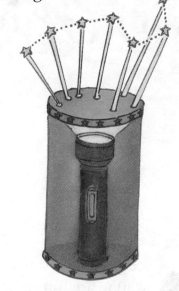

3. Show your constellation to others. Tell them about your constellation. Put on a star show with friends who have made their own constellation boxes.

More to Try: Learn American Indian or native Hawaiian stories about the movement of the stars. Share what you learn with your group.

TRY IT!

SPORTS AND GAMES

Skating

Ice skating and roller skating are fun sports and are good for fitness. Always skate with a buddy and follow safety rules.

You will need:

- A pair of skates
- Comfortable clothes
- Safety items—knee pads, wrist guards, etc.

1. Practice falling. Stand in your skates and bend your knees so that you are squatting. Bend backward a little and fall on your bottom. Extend your arms in front of you.

2. Skate forward, to your left, to your right, around corners, and stop.

3. Skate backwards, to your left, to your right, around corners, and stop.

4. Skate forward and backward to music with a partner.

Ball Games

Many sports are played with balls. Try these exercises with at least two kinds of round balls, such as a baseball and a basketball. You'll also need this book. Practice each of these steps.

1. Toss the ball back and forth from your right hand to your left hand.

2. Bounce the ball with your right hand, then with your left hand.

3. Throw the ball in the air and catch it with two hands.

Bicycling

Bicycling is fun and good exercise. If you have a bicycle, try these bicycling skills.

1. Ride as slowly as you can without stopping.

2. Ride in circles. Try to make the circles as small as you can.

3. Ride in a long, straight line.

4. Practice turning, using hand signals. To turn left, put your left arm straight out with the palm forward. To turn right, put your left arm out and bent upwards at the elbow, with fingers pointing up. To stop, put your left arm out and bent down at the elbow, with fingers pointing down.

5. Set up a bicycling practice course. Place 10–20 large metal cans in a wide play area. Try to ride around the course without touching the cans.

Swimming

Have an adult teach you how to swim. Always remember the following rules:

- Have an adult watch you.
- Swim with a buddy.
- Swim where there are a lifeguard and rescue equipment.
- Leave the water before you get tired or cold.

You will need:

- A swimsuit
- Water (pool, beach, or lake)
- An adult to watch

Ask the adult to help you practice these swimming skills.

1. Sit down in knee-deep water with feet and legs in front of you and hands behind you on the bottom. Move your head back slightly. Straighten your legs and raise your feet.

2. Kneel in water up to your knees. Hold your friend's hand for balance. Put your head into the water and see if you can hold your breath while you count to ten. See if you can keep your eyes open when underwater.

3. See how long you can tread water. Move your arms and legs underwater. Keep your head above the water and your body straight.

Games

Look through this book and find some games you'd like to teach others. Find at least two and teach them to someone else.

Paper Kick Ball

Your feet are very important for many sports and games. Try this football game with your friends.

You will need:

- 1 large brown paper bag
- 4 or more players

1. Press the brown paper bag into a ball.

2. All the players stand in a circle.

3. Choose one player to be the first kicker.

4. The first kicker kicks the paper ball to someone she names in the circle.

5. The ball keeps getting kicked until someone misses it and it goes outside the circle.

6. The person who missed the ball gets a point. She then kicks the ball to someone else.

7. The winner is the player with the lowest number of points.

WATER EVERYWHERE

Find out about water without getting wet.

Made of Water

Water is part of more things than you may think. It's even part of you! Your body has more water in it than any other substance.

Water mixes with other things so that it often doesn't look like water—milk and orange juice are two examples. Try to find food containers that list water as an ingredient. Make a list. Work with friends.

Drip Drop

Read the section called "Conservation" on pages 147–148. Find a faucet that leaks around your house, school, camp, or neighborhood park. Put a measure under it and time how long it takes to fill up. How many cups or even gallons are wasted in a day at this site? See if you can get someone to fix the faucet or learn how to fix it with someone who knows how to make the repair.

Clean, Clear Water

Do a taste test using water from the tap, distilled water, and bottled spring water. Can you taste a difference? Where does the tap water come from in your home, at your school, and at your camp?

Try this, *but no taste tests!*

1. Do some simple tests using coffee filters and a funnel. Gather some water samples from mud puddles, standing water, a lake or a stream, the tap, and other sources.

2. Write in pencil on the edge of each filter the name of your water source. Strain that water through the filter.

3. Compare filter papers. Are there differences among them?

Water Snooper

To build a water snooper, you will need:

- A large can
- Clear plastic wrap
- Rubber bands

1. Have someone help you remove both ends of the large can.

2. Take the plastic wrap and put it on one end of the can.

3. Hold it in place with the rubber bands.

4. Use the snooper to look into a pond or tide pool, or an aquarium or puddle, by submerging the end with the plastic into your water.

More to Try: Make a water-drop magnifying lens. Take a piece of clear plastic wrap and put two or three drops of water in the middle of it. Hold the plastic over the letters in this book. Are they larger? Hold the plastic over other objects.

Water Explorer

Visit a pond, lake, small stream, or a protected tide pool with your troop or with an organized group. Look for creatures and plants that live in the water.

You will need:
- A strainer
- A white plastic bowl with water in it

1. Dip the strainer in the water and empty what you find into the white plastic bowl that has water in it.

2. If you find living things, how do they move?

3. Look under rocks in the water. Do creatures hide under them or cling to them?

4. Remember to leave the area as you found it. Just use the water snooper to see into the water.

More to Try: Visit an aquarium. Create an aquarium with pond water and draw the changes that take place over several weeks.

Water Layers

You can see that salt water is different than fresh water in more ways than taste.

You will need:

- 2 glasses
- Warm water
- Container of salt
- Food coloring or ink
- Spoon
- Measuring cup

1. Put one cup of water in a glass. Slowly add salt. Keep stirring. Stop when salt won't dissolve and stays at the bottom.

2. Add some food coloring or ink to the salty water.

3. Hold the spoon to the top of the water and very slowly pour one cup of fresh water onto the spoon. The fresh water will stay on top, because it is not as heavy as salt water.

More to Try: Do this experiment in reverse. Add salt water to fresh water. Try adding cold salty water to warm fresh water.

BRIDGE TO JUNIOR GIRL SCOUTS PATCH

As a Brownie Girl Scout, you have fun, make friends, and learn new things. At the end of your last year in Brownie Girl Scouting, you can look forward to Junior Girl Scouting! To help you become a Junior Girl Scout, you may take part in bridging activities that will help you learn all about Junior Girl Scouting.

To earn the Bridge to Junior Girl Scouts patch, you must do at least one activity from each of the seven bridging steps in the order that they are numbered. You and your leader can also decide on special things to do for each step.

Seven Bridging Steps

Bridging Step 1:
Find Out About Junior Girl Scouting

- Invite a Junior Girl Scout to tell you about Junior Girl Scouting.
- Invite an adult who works with Junior Girl Scouts to tell you about Junior Girl Scouting. Find out how you can become a Junior Girl Scout.
- Find a Junior Girl Scout to be your "big sister" and help you with bridging activities.
- Look at the uniform and recognitions for Junior Girl Scouts.

Bridging Step 2:
Do a Junior Girl Scout Activity

- Do a Junior Girl Scout badge activity from a badge with a green background in *Girl Scout Badges and Signs*.
- Do an activity from the *Junior Girl Scout Handbook*. (You may do a badge activity from the badges at the back of the handbook.)
- Make something described in the *Junior Girl Scout Handbook*.

Bridging Step 3:
Do Something with a Junior Girl Scout

- Go on a field trip.
- Do a service project.
- Make something, using your camping skills.
- Make some food to share with other girls.
- Find and write to a Junior Girl Scout pen pal who lives in your area or another state. Ask your local Girl Scout council representative for help.

Bridging Step 4:
Share What You Learn About Junior Girl Scouting with Brownie or Daisy Girl Scouts

- Make a collage about Junior Girl Scouting for your Brownie or Daisy Girl Scout friends.
- Show them a Junior Girl Scout activity.
- Tell them about a field trip or service project that you did with a Junior Girl Scout.
- Teach them a song or game that you learned from a Junior Girl Scout.

Bridging Step 5:
Do Junior Girl Scout Recognitions Activities

- Earn a Dabbler badge from one of the worlds of interest in *Girl Scout Badges and Signs.*
- Earn a badge with a green background from *Girl Scout Badges and Signs.*

- Do a badge activity from each world of interest in *Girl Scout Badges and Signs.*
- Do one activity from five different badges in the *Junior Girl Scout Handbook.*

Bridging Step 6:
Help Plan Your Bridging (Fly-Up) Ceremony

- Learn how to do an opening or closing for a ceremony that is different from any opening or closing you have done before.

- Write a poem about Brownie or Junior Girl Scouting.
- Make up a song for the ceremony.
- Design and make invitations for the ceremony.
- Make decorations to be used at the ceremony.

Bridging Step 7:
Plan and Do a Summer
Girl Scout Activity

If your Girl Scout group has its Court of Awards before summer, you may be able to get your Bridge to Junior Girl Scouts patch then. Remember to promise to do Step 7 over the summer.

- Go to Girl Scout camp.
- Plan and go on a picnic with some other Girl Scouts.
- Have a campfire or cookout with other Girl Scouts.
- Make a summer scrapbook to share with your new Junior Girl Scout friends.
- Have a sports day with other Girl Scouts.
- Plan a get-acquainted activity that you can do in the fall with your new Junior Girl Scout friends.
- Write a summer newsletter to send to other Girl Scouts.
- Do a service project.

Looking Back and Looking Ahead

Brownie Girl Scouts who become Junior Girl Scouts receive Brownie Girl Scout wings that they can wear as Junior Girl Scouts. Girls who join Junior Girl Scouting without first being Brownie Girl Scouts do not receive Brownie Girl Scout wings. They may ask you about your wings. Do you know how they got their name?

A long time ago, Brownie Girl Scout leaders were called "Brown Owls." Remember the Wise Owl in the Brownie story? At the fly-up ceremony, the Brown Owl gave wings to those girls in her troop who were ready to go to the next age level in Girl Scouting.

At a fly-up ceremony, you receive your wings and renew your Girl Scout Promise and you get the membership pin that is worn by Junior, Cadette, Senior, and adult

Helping Others Learn About Girl Scouting

Now that you know how much fun Girl Scouting can be, why not tell your friends about it! You can help others learn about Girl Scouting by:

- Making a poster for Girl Scout Week showing things you do as a Brownie Girl Scout.
- Helping in a flag ceremony at a neighborhood or council event.
- Bringing a friend to a Girl Scouting event.
- Helping to get a Girl Scout camp ready for a summer season.

Girl Scouts. You will have a chance to plan your fly-up ceremony with the girls in your troop and with the Junior Girl Scouts in the troop you will be joining.

Each step of Junior Girl Scouting can be filled with fun and adventure. There are badges and signs you can work on as a Junior Girl Scout, or you can invent your own badge and develop an "Our Own Troop's" badge. You can also earn the Junior Aide patch by helping Brownie Girl Scouts bridge to Junior Girl Scouting. The *Junior Girl Scout Handbook* has a lot of information and fun activities for you and your Junior Girl Scout friends. The possibilities are many!

Brownie Girl Scout Memories

Your copy of the *Brownie Girl Scout Handbook* can be a record of all the fun times you had and of all the new things you learned as a Brownie Girl Scout. Think of the new friends you made. What will you remember most about being a Brownie Girl Scout? Use this space for friends' autographs, special memories, or your own special thoughts.

Index

Adinkra cloth, 91–92
Aerobics, 191–192
Age of Girl Scouts, 12, 30
Air pollution and quality, 146, 195
Alita Girl Guides (Peru), 94–98
Alphabet code, 217
Ananse Guides (Ghana), 88–92
Andersen, Hans Christian, 99
Animals, 9, 192–193
Arapaho Nation, story from, 106–107

Backpacks, 151–152
Baden-Powell, Sir Robert, 10, 25
Ball games, 272
Balloons, blowing up, 134–135
Batik, 94
Beads, 174
Bicycling, 273
Blind walk, 77
Blizzards, 140
Bluebird Girl Guides (Thailand), 92–94
Board Tic Tac Toe (game), 47
Body care, 36–42
Box game, 81
Brain power, 128–132, 228
Bridge to Brownie Girl Scouts patch, 29
Bridging, 31, 278–282
Brownie Girl Scouts. *See also specific topics*
    around the world, 88–100, 169

getting involved in, 115
    naming of, 17–21
Bubbles, making, 258
Butterfly, chemical, 134–135

Cadette Girl Scouts, 30
Camping, 148–149, 157–160, 234
Careers, 67–68, 178–179
Ceremonies, 23–24, 202
Checks, 132
Chemistry, 133–135, 260–261
Choices, making, 182
Circle glider, making, 222
Circles, Brownie Girl Scout, 120
Citizenship, 115–117, 182–183
Clothes, 172, 199
    caring for, 42–44
    uniforms, 26–27
    weather and, 44, 151
Clouds, 139–140
Color and light, 136–137
Colors and shapes mobile, 185
Computers, 125–127, 129–130, 255–256
Conservation, 147–148, 275
Cookies, Girl Scout, sale of, 122
Cooking, 158, 197–198, 207
"Coyote and the Moon" (story), 104–105
Credit cards, 132
Crystals, making, 258

Daisy Girl Scouts, 12, 30–31
Dance, 192
Denmark, Grønsmutte Girl Scouts in, 98–100
Disabilities, 77, 177
Dolls, yarn, making, 249
Dough art, 134
Dough shapes, making, 186

Eating right, 39–41
Ecology hunt, 237
Edith Macy Conference Center, 32
Electricity, 143, 148, 261
Emergencies, 52, 152
Endangered animals, 168
Energy, 148, 223, 255
Environment, 144–148, 194–199
Erosion, 194
Evaporation, 138, 240
Exercise, 42, 191–193
Exploring
    neighborhoods, 85
    outdoors, 156–157
    space, 269–271
    water, 276–277
Eye changes, 228

Face painting, 172–173
Family, 70–75, 170
Feelings, 65, 181
Fingerprints, 228
Finger weaving, 96
Fire safety, 54–56, 158, 252
First aid, 58–62, 253
Fitness wheel, 229–230
Fliers, making, 221
Food
    around the world, 100, 170

eating right and, 39–41
    for outdoors, 152–153, 156, 158–159, 239
Food chain, 245
Food pyramid, 39, 201
Fossil prints, 240
Friends, 75–83
    with different abilities, 75–79
    learning to be, 79–81
    school and, 82–83
    scrapbook about, 181
    things to do with, 81–82
Friendship circle, 22
Friendship squeeze, 22
Frost, 140
Frostbite, 60–61

Games, 47, 81–82, 154, 213, 236, 274
    around the world, 99–101, 171, 243, 246–247
Garbage, 146–147, 199
Gas, 133
Ghana, Ananse Guides in, 88–92
Girl Scouting (Girl Scouts), 7–13
    ceremonies of, 23–24, 202
    special days for, 24–25, 202
    special ways of, 22–23, 202
Goal setting, 117–118
Government, troop, 119–120
Greek mosaics, 102
Grønsmutte Girl Scouts (Denmark), 98–100

Habitat hunt, 155
Handshake, Girl Scout, 22
Hawk and Hens (game), 101, 247
Heat exhaustion, 60
Hiking, 154, 234
Home, safety at, 48–49, 52–54

Home care, 44–47, 175
Hourglass, making, 130–131
Hurricanes, 140
Hypothermia, 60

Inca, 96–97
Initials (game), 81
Insignia and recognitions, 28–29. *See also* Try-Its
Instruments, making, 266–268
Interests and talents, 66–67, 210
Investiture, 31
Invisible ink, 134

Jan-ken-pon (game), 101, 247
Jigsaw puzzles, 233
Juliette Gordon Low Girl Scout National Center
    ("The Birthplace"), 32
Junior Girl Scouts, 30, 278–282

Kazoo, making, 268
Kim's Game, 246
Kite festival, 93
Kite flying, 222–223
Knee jerk, 229
Knots, 159, 174, 237

Landfill, making, 199
Language, 98, 243
Law and Promise, Girl Scout, 14–15
Laws, 182
Leadership, 111–124
    citizenship and, 115–117
    goal setting and, 117–118
    group planning and, 123–124

troop government and, 119–120
    troop money and, 121–122
Leaf hunt, 244
Light and color, 136–137
Lightning, 140, 142–143
Lip protection, 152
Liquids, 133
Looms, making, 97–98
Low, Juliette Gordon (Daisy), 8–12, 24, 202

Magnets, 135–136, 261
Manners, 214–215
Marionettes, 251
Masks, making, 174
Matter, 133
Measuring, 129–132, 256
Melody glasses, 226
Membership star, 29
Messages, composing, 190
Mexican yarn painting, 188
Mexico, clay birds from, 102
Mini-environment, making, 144
Minimum impact, 150, 152
Mirror image, 79
Mr. Bear (game), 101, 247
Mobius strips, 232
Money, 121–122, 131–132
Moon, 131, 269
Mosaics, Greek, 102
Motto, Girl Scout, 23
Muscle reaction, 229
Music for instruments, composing, 190

National centers, 32
Neighbors (neighborhood), 84–86, 155, 175, 183, 234

Oil spills, 145, 196
Origami, 231–232
Outdoor skills and adventures, 16, 148–160
    camping, 148–149, 234
    clothes, 150–152
    day packs, 151–152
    exploring, 156–157
    meet out, 152–154
    move out, 154–155
    planning, 150, 156
    safety, 150, 153
    use your senses in, 153–154, 238

Paper, making, 259–260
Paper kick ball, 274
Papier-mâché, 173–174
Parks and play areas, safety in, 49, 252–253
Parties, 215
Patches, 29. *See also* Insignia and recognitions; Try-Its
People. *See also* Family; Friends; Neighbors
    around the world, 87–107, 169–171, 243
    different from you, 108–110, 181
    meeting, 215
Peru, Alita Girl Guides in, 94–98
Phone calls, 152, 214
Pin of Brownie Girl Scouts, 28
Plants, 195, 244–245
Plays, composing, 190
Pocket knife, use of, 235
Poems, composing, 189
Pollution, 144–147, 195
Prints, fossil, 240
Promise and Law, Girl Scout, 14–15
Pulse, 229
Puppets, 72
    finger, 248

paper-bag, 250
stage for, 250

Rabbit Without a House (game), 100–101
Rain, 139–140, 240
Rain poncho, 152
Recycling, 145–147, 199, 259–260
Rededication, 31
Red Light, Green Light (game), 246
Reflexes, 228–229
Repairs, home, 46–47
Ring, Brownie Girl Scout, 22, 119–120
Rockets, making, 270–271
Rocks, 242
Rubbings, 154, 239

Safety, 48–57, 250. *See also* Suzy Safety
    cooking and, 158
    do's and don'ts of, 48
    emergencies and, 52
    fire, 54–56, 252
    first aid and, 58–62, 253
    outdoor skills and adventures and, 150, 153
    with people you know, 50–51
    quiz on, 57
    sports, 56
    weather and, 142–143
    on your own at home, 52–54
Savings accounts, 132
Schools, friends and, 82–83
Science, 132–148
    chemistry and, 133–135, 260–261
    conservation and, 147–148
    light and color, 136–137
    magnets, 135–136

pollution and, 144–147
weather and, 137–143
Seed hunt, 155
Seed race, 241
Seed sprout, 244
Senior Girl Scouts, 30
Sheep and Hyena (game), 247
Shelter, 167
Sign, Girl Scout, 22
Sign language, 77–79, 265
Signs, trail, 157, 237
Sit-upons, 152, 204
Skating, 272
Sky watcher, 195
Sleeping bags, 160
Slogan, Girl Scout, 23
Sloppy joes, making, 201
S'mores, making, 203
Snacks, 41, 152, 156, 200–201, 239
Snow, 140
Soil, 194
Solar cookers, making, 197–198
Solids, 133
Songs, 243. *See also* Music
　　Brownie Friend-Maker Song, 226–227
　　Brownie Smile Song, 24
　　composing, 189
　　feeling good about yourself, 62–64
　　Los Maizales, 95
　　Make New Friends, 163
Soup, Brownie, 207
Sports, 56, 272–274
Stars, 271
Static antics, 143
Stencil stampers, 184–185
Storms, 140, 142–143
Storytelling, 7–11, 17–21, 33–35, 69–71, 88–90, 99, 104–108,
　　125–127, 243, 271

Sun, 138
Sunscreen, 152
Suzy Safety, 13, 53, 199, 203, 254, 264, 276
Swimming, 273

Talking signal, 120
Tapatan (game), 171
Terrariums, making, 196–197
Thailand, Bluebird Girl Guides in, 92–94
Thermometers, use of, 195
Thunderstorms, 140, 142
Tie-dyeing, 103
Time
　　measuring, 256
　　telling, 130–131
Tornadoes, 140, 142–143
Trail signs, 157, 237
Trash busters, 199
Trees, 154, 244
T-shirt art, 172
Twig rafts, making, 224

Uniforms, 26–27

Water bottle, 152
Weather, 221, 240
Weaving, 96–98, 186–187
Weird glop, making, 133–134
Whistle, 152
Wind, 138, 241–242
Windbreaker, 152
Wind wheels, 220–221
"Woman with Eight Children, The" (story), 106–107
World centers, 32
Worlds of interest, 16
World Trefoil pin, 28

Program 3/93